Knit It Together

Patterns and Inspiration
for Knitting Circles

Suzyn Jackson, Editor

Voyageur Press

Acknowledgments

I could not have put this book together without the help of many people along the way. My first thanks have to go to Rosemary and David Jackson, for tromping all over Calgary to find an art gallery that was featuring the Revolutionary Knitting Circle. My friends Rachel Cottone, Wilma Perry, and Mary Stein are the queens of networking. I am always grateful to Stephen I. Silberfein for his proofreading services.

Props to the members of the Columbia Sip & Knit group, for gamely laughing through a chilly March photo shoot: Denise Ciotti, Cassie Coddington, Dorothy D'Ascanio, Cathy Frantz, Bridget K. Fredstrom, Jacqueline Gutenkunst, Ellen King, Vivian Rexroad, and Debbi Spranza.

Huge thanks and kudos to the amazing folks from all over the continent who knitted leaves for the Tree of Life Banner. Thank you Denise Ciotti, Connie Clark, Cassie Coddington, Kelly Conrad, Janet Cottone, Elizabeth Cowley, Marg Godin, Ellen King, April Klick, Debbie McGahen, Diane Vollmer, Shirley Worth, and Arwyn Yarwood-Hoeppner. Thanks to London Nelson and Elizabeth Wrobel for helping to knit the friendship scarves, to Charlotte Quiggle for putting the finishing touches on the New Skills Blanket, and to Margret Aldrich, Anitra Budd, Cindi Dean, Lindsay Haas, and LeAnn Kuhlman for their help with the photos on page 33 and page 102.

My editors, Kari Cornell and Charlotte Quiggle, guided me with tact and grace. I am grateful to them for their no-nonsense professionalism, their imaginative ideas, and their deep knowledge.

My thanks go out to the circle of contributors—writers, designers, and photographers—who created this book. This book is about the power of groups, and you definitely put this idea into action.

Finally, I must thank my family. To my mother: Thank you for always believing in me. To my husband, Alvaro J. Gonzalez: Thank you for your lyrical eye and rock-steady support. And to my sons: Thank you for being my joy and my inspiration.

First published in 2009 by Voyageur Press, an imprint of MBI Publishing Company, 400 First Avenue North, Suite 300, Minneapolis, MN 55401 USA

Voyageur Press titles are also available at discounts in bulk quantity for industrial or sales-promotional use. For details write to Special Sales Manager at MBI Publishing Company, 400 First Avenue North, Suite 300, Minneapolis, MN 55401 USA.

To find out more about our books, visit us online at www.voyageurpress.com.

Editor: Kari Cornell
Designer: Sara Holle
Jacket Designer: Greg Nettles

Printed in China

Library of Congress Cataloging-in-Publication Data
Knit it together : patterns and inspiration for knitting circles / Suzyn Jackson, editor.
  p. cm.
Includes bibliographical references and index.
ISBN 978-0-7603-3073-9 (sb : alk. paper)
1. Knitting. 2. Knitters (Persons) I. Jackson, Suzyn, 1974–
TT825.K62875 2009
746.43'2041—dc22
                                           2008035943

Contents

Introduction

I set out to assemble this book using the widest possible definition of a knitting circle: more than one knitter, period. Like any good knitting circle, I welcomed a wide range of people. Some contributors are established writers and designers, while for others this represents their first published work. The variety of voices and visions is fascinating, much like a lively group of knitters, gabbing and clicking away.

I also started with an idea for collaborative knitting projects, projects specifically designed to be knit by a group. Using the varied skills and talents of a group of knitters, these projects have a richness and texture not usually found in solo ventures. The finished pieces embody the spirit of the group. The only difficulty is deciding who gets to keep them! (I suggest knitting them as gifts.)

Encountering other knitters is a sure way to expand your concept of what is possible in the world of knitting. A good knitting library can do the same thing. These days, books aren't the only places to find new ideas; the Internet has vast resources for knitters. Throughout this book, I have included knitting books, websites, and organizations to inspire your future knitting adventures.

While I hope you will find a sense of community among these pages that will remind you of a knitting circle, this book is not a learn-to-knit book, and it is not meant to be a substitute for a knitting class. New knitters are welcome, of course, and there are patterns here that beginners can comfortably tackle, but for the nitty-gritty how-to stuff, please refer to the list of recommended technique books provided on page 133.

So, welcome to my knitting circle: a collection of writers and designers who have thought deeply about how a community of knitters with a shared passion for yarn and needles can bridge divides, spread goodwill, and strengthen us all.

Chapter One
Beginnings

A young Italian girl strolls and knits in *Villanella*, an engraving by J. Levasseur based on an 1874 painting by C. H. Jalabert.

A Stroll through Knitting Circles Past

by Suzyn Jackson

Knitting is a relative newcomer to the craft scene. When Moses was discovered in a basket, he wasn't wearing knitted booties. And if Penelope had been knitting instead of weaving as she waited for Odysseus to come home, she could have gone over to a friend's house for a good chat-and-rip session. In fact, there are no references to knitting in ancient texts, because knitting hadn't been invented yet.

Beginnings: Mysteries and Guilds

One of the earliest examples of true knitting is an intricately patterned cushion found in northern Spain in the tomb of Fernando de la Cerda, who died in 1275. The cushion is covered with heraldic symbols. Arabic letters worked into the pattern suggest that the knitter might have been Muslim, albeit working for a Christian prince. Other exquisite and rare examples of early knitting include pillows, gloves, and socks, but there is no record of who knitted them.

The first known knitting circles were capknitters' guilds, established throughout Europe in the fifteenth and sixteenth centuries. These knitters were considered master craftsmen, and making and selling caps required a license. Thanks to the industriousness of the guild, caps were the first mass-produced knitted garments. They were floppy, like berets with brims, knitted in the round (the purl stitch was not yet known) and felted. The patterns were closely guarded guild secrets. As Elizabethan fashions eventually reached ridiculous extremes, caps followed suit, developing slashing to show off a colorful lining, or even multiple brims that made the caps look like a stack of pancakes.

A style popular with soldiers originated in Wales and was called a "Monmouth cap." These caps, which resembled modern toques, were worn as padding under metal helmets. The soldiers of Shakespeare's *Henry V* wore them, replete with leeks worn as a symbol of Welsh pride: ". . . the Welshmen did good service in a garden where leeks did grow, wearing leeks in their Monmouth caps . . . I do believe your majesty takes no scorn to wear the leek upon Saint Tavy's day."

Knitting as Industry and Drudgery

Capknitters' monopoly of the craft ended in the mid-sixteenth century, thanks to two developments: the invention of wire and the popularity of knitted stockings. It is said that the young Elizabeth I received a gift of knitted silk stockings and declared that she would wear no more cloth stockings. Silk stockings from France and Spain were soon the height of English fashion.

In this eighteenth-century painting by an unknown artist, a mother knits socks while her daughter looks on.

Around the same time, the first mechanized wireworks was founded in England. Until then, steel knitting needles were difficult to make and prohibitively expensive. Steel wire was comparatively cheap. Suddenly, anyone could pick up a few lengths of wire and start knitting. (The knitting needles we use today, with helpful features such as pointy tips and knobs on the ends, would not appear for a couple of centuries.)

Not everyone could afford silk stockings, of course. But England had plenty of sheep, and it turned out that English wool made better stocking yarn than the wool produced on the continent. As well as being a cheaper imitation of courtly fashion, knitted woolen stockings were much more comfortable than the cloth leggings—cut on the bias—that most people wore at that time. Affordable, warm, and fashionable, woolen stockings were a hit! By the end of Elizabeth I's reign, knitted woolen stockings had become a major English industry. Not only were the new stockings worn by most English people, but thousands of pairs of stockings were shipped from England to Europe every year.

Industry on this scale was beyond the scope of a guild. Knitting quickly shifted from a master craft to the incessant drudgery of the poor. Everyone knitted, all the time—while walking, when riding in oxcarts, or by firelight in the evening. Special schools were established to teach knitting to boys and girls as young as five. Even at that age, poor children were expected to contribute to the household income by knitting.

Stockings were neither quick nor easy to knit. Both the wool and the wires were fine, making for a huge number of tiny stitches. The oldest extant English knitting pattern, printed in 1655 (as a single sentence, three pages long), calls for casting on six score and twelve, or 132 stitches—more than most adult sweaters call for these days. An accomplished adult knitter could make six pairs of stockings a week!

Around the end of the sixteenth century, William Lee invented the knitting frame. Elizabeth I denied him a patent, as the machine threatened the livelihood of an entire economic class. Not until England's Commonwealth period was the Framework Knitters' Guild granted a charter of incorporation, on July 13, 1657. As machine knitting increased in quality and decreased in price, handknitting for profit slowly but inevitably died out. Eventually, the only people knitting stockings were those who could not afford to buy machine-knitted ones for their families.

Knitting in the New World

English Puritans railed against the frills and fancy colors of haute couture Elizabethan knitted stockings, but they took their knitting wires with them when they sailed to the New World in the early seventeenth century. Knitting fit well into the Puritan idea that idleness was an unforgivable sin. Any opportunity to sit down and rest was an opportunity to take up one's knitting—even shepherds were expected to knit while watching their sheep.

Knitting was both a necessity and a social accomplishment in colonial America, and the work was often shared in informal knitting circles called "bees." These bees served a dual purpose: The colonists could socialize while continuing the endless work of maintaining a family in the New World. Whether they regarded idleness as a sin or a luxury, early colonists simply could not afford the time to go visiting without taking along some sort of work, and knitting was easily portable.

Colonial society eventually became established enough that the wealthy could afford some leisure, but by then knitting was firmly entrenched in American culture, and fancy stitchwork was considered essential in a wealthy young lady's education. Anything imported held particular cachet. Schools advertised instruction in the latest European knitting methods, but the most fashionable (and well-off) colonists purchased knitted goods imported from England.

By the mid-eighteenth century, after several costly wars, the English government was desperate for money. It began to require (and increasingly tax) the purchase of English goods in the colonies. The American spirit of independence (or, one could say, indignation) arose. In resistance to the Stamp Tax of 1765, colonial women boycotted English goods, resolving to clothe their families in "naught but homespun." Spinning and knitting bees became a mania, as women realized that their domestic pursuits had political implications.

Bees, previously simple social occasions, became women's form of civil outcry. Women flocked to public spaces—often churches and vicars' homes—where they spun and knit all day. Their industry fed the belief that Americans could survive independent of Britain, sustaining themselves as a new country. The English governors underestimated colonial self-sufficiency and were surprised to learn that they needed the colonies more than the colonies needed them.

In this reproduction of the painting *Washington, Our First War Time Knitter*, Martha Washington knits during the American Revolution. *Library of Congress*

Knitting Moves up the Class Structure

In eighteenth- and early nineteenth-century Europe, knitting was not fashionable, and it was practiced mainly by the lower classes. Only two women in Jane Austen's novels knit. Mrs. Smith of *Persuasion* takes up knitting as a part of her recovery from a rheumatic fever following her husband's death, and she must be taught by her nurse, a member of a lower class. "As soon as I could use my hands she taught me to knit, which has been a great amusement; and she put me in the way of making these

KNIT A BIT
FOR OUR FIRST LINE OF DEFENSE
WOOL, NEEDLES AND DIRECTIONS
Comforts Committee of the Navy League
OF THE UNITED STATES
509 FIFTH AVENUE, NEW YORK CITY

In this poster from the World War I era, the Comforts Committee of the Navy League of the United States promotes knitting as the "first line of defense" on the homefront. *Library of Congress*

little thread-cases, pin-cushions and card-racks, which you always find me so busy about. . . ."

It was in the drawing rooms of the mid-nineteenth century that, for the first time, the act of knitting became fashionable in England. The soft, richly dyed Merino wool being imported from Germany spurred this trend, and the fact that the young Queen Victoria knitted also helped. Knitting books appeared for the first time, and though the instructions were vague and poorly edited (gauge and needle size were almost never mentioned), they were hugely popular. They included patterns for tiny decorative objects, baby clothes, counterpanes (a type of knitted quilt), purses, and pincushions, as well as more practical mittens, gloves, and shawls. The fine ladies of English drawing rooms did not knit stockings, nor were they particularly concerned with speed. In the name of "elegance," they adopted an awkward method of holding the right-hand needle like a pen. After centuries of knitting for gain, warmth, and independence, these women knitted simply to pass the time.

Some ladies knitted "comforts" for their coachmen, such as mittens, scarves, and socks; thus knitting for charity was born. It did not thrive, however. Upper-class Victorians were concerned that "indulging" the poor would encourage sloth, and they were more likely to "help" by organizing work programs or sometimes paying poor women to knit. Most of the time, when fashionable ladies were inspired to knit for others, knitting for soldiers was considered most appropriate.

Knitting through Revolution and War

The most notorious of all knitting circles, *Les Tricoteuses*, were famous for attending the beheadings of the French Revolution with their knitting in tow. These real women inspired Dickens' account of starving Parisian knitters in *A Tale of Two Cities*: "All the women knitted. They knitted worthless things; but, the mechanical work was a mechanical substitute for eating and drinking. . . . So much was closing in about the women who sat knitting, knitting, that they their very selves were closing in around a structure yet unbuilt, where they were to sit knitting, knitting, counting dropping heads." Dickens implies that the bloodthirst—and the knitting—was pervasive throughout Paris, that women from all quarters were clamoring for the heads of the nobility. While knitting was still common among the lower classes at the time, the real Tricoteuses were a small group. The Commune of Paris organized and paid these particularly sadistic women to attend tribunals and beheadings. Their job, in the words of the Commune decree, was "to greet death, to insult the victims, and to glut their eyes with blood." They did their job well, jeering and shrieking as the upper classes were led to their death, knitting through it all.

If the French can claim the most notorious knitting circle of all time, the Union women of the American Civil War can claim the largest: the United States Sanitary Commission, established on April 21, 1861. Understanding that it would be almost impossible to get desperately needed gifts of clothing and food directly to their family members, the women of the North united to provide food and clothing to *every* Union soldier. The organization involved was mind-boggling, with more than 750 Soldier's Aid chapters formed in the first year alone. In addition to knitting and sewing, the women ran "Sanitary Fairs" to raise funds. Their operating budget for the entire war topped $5 million—an almost inconceivable sum in that era.

Knitting for soldiers became a sadly recurrent pursuit. The women of England first knitted for their soldiers in the Crimean and Boer wars. The women of America knitted through the American Revolutionary and Civil wars. Women in America, Canada, England, and throughout Europe knitted for their soldiers through both World Wars. At home, often with no news of their loved ones for months or years, women gathered to knit in formal meetings and informal groups. They worked their anxiety and love into their craft, hoping that their socks, scarves, and mittens would warm both bodies and hearts.

College students gather together to knit in the early 1950s. *Library of Congress*

More Recent Times: Knitting for Fun and Fashion

The twentieth century brought both improvements in machine-knitting technology and the rise of knitwear in the world of fashion. While people were more likely to wear knitted clothing, the clothing was less likely to be handmade. Knitting for any purpose other than pleasure became rare.

There were exceptions, of course. The Great Depression of the 1930s hit the mining region of Bohuslän, Sweden, particularly hard. A group of women from the region, with the help of the governor's wife, formed Bohus Stickning (Bohus Knitting). Starting with simple gloves and socks, they eventually commissioned designers and ran knitting courses, building a thriving handicraft industry. By the 1950s, intricately patterned Bohus sweaters not only supported the community, but were considered the height of fashion and a necessity for the well-dressed Swede.

Handknitting waned in popularity through most of the twentieth century, only to experience a resurgence toward the end. Today, some groups of knitters gather in local coffee shops, while others gather from around the world in online "knitalongs." In wealthy nations, knitting for charity is popular, while in poorer countries, women are forming collectives to sell their hand-knits in world markets and rebuilding their communities in the process.

Why do we gather with others to knit together? To warm body and soul, certainly. For profit, sometimes. As a creative act, often. To help others, or pass the time? Both, of course. The breadth and variety of knitters past is reflected in the knitting circles of today. In this relatively young craft, we're only getting started.

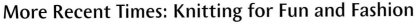

For More on the History of Knitting

Want to learn more about the history of knitting? The following books cover the craft from its earliest artifacts to the present day.

A History of Hand Knitting by Richard Rutt, published by Interweave Press, Inc., 1987

Knitting America: A Glorious Heritage from Warm Socks to High Art by Susan M. Strawn, published by Voyageur Press, 2007

No Idle Hands: The Social History of American Knitting by Anne L. Macdonald, published by Ballantine Books, 1988

Poems of Color: Knitting in the Bohus Tradition by Wendy Keele, published by Interweave Press, 1995

How to Knit Together a Group in Eight Easy Steps

by Kelley Dean-Crowley

Five years ago, I knitted a handful of women together into a group that laughs, chats, has tea, and even knits together. The group, although small, has kept on throughout that time, swelling to twenty people, though occasionally there is a night when life gets in the way and no one can make it at all. On a quiet night, we cover the gamut of conversation from work, school, and relationships to the things you should never discuss in groups—religion, politics, and sex. There have been times when new interests have lured me away from knitting for a short while, but nothing has pulled me away from Wednesday night yet.

Interested in starting a knitting circle in your area? Here are the steps that I followed to create mine.

Find Any Existing Knitting Groups in Your Area

This may seem illogical if you have already decided to start a knitting group, but there is always something to learn from this process. When I was looking to start my group, knowing where other groups met gave me ideas for where my group could meet.

Set Your Objective

Of course, your objective is to create a knitting group. But will any knitting group do? Would you like sock knitters or shawl knitters or maybe machine knitters? Are you willing to teach newbies, or would you prefer that all members know the basics? The clearer your objective, the easier it will be to find other knitters who share your goal.

If You Spread the Word, They Will Come

Put it out there. I turned to the online community Knitter's Review for local members, and, sure enough, a handful of knitters expressed interest. I have since posted the group to a variety of lists, groups, and websites to help people find us. Consider posting to other craft or knitting forums, local bulletin boards, the local library, local schools, craigslist.org, or social networking websites. Don't forget the local yarn and craft stores. Determine whether there is interest, and how much, and collect contact information to use later.

Set a Date

How often will the group meet? When will you meet and how long will meetings last? What day and time is convenient for most? It will be virtually impossible to find a day and time that works for everyone, all the time, and, as groups get larger, the odds of everyone being available get even smaller. Acknowledge this and go for the day and time when most can meet.

Location, Location, Location

You will need a place that is easily accessible, is comfortable, can support your group, and, most important, would like to have you. My group meets at a local branch of a large chain bookstore. They carry more knitting books than most bookstores and have comfortable chairs, a café, and staff who now love to see us every Wednesday. Before I talked to the manager of this bookstore, I approached a local bookstore—their competition—and was not even politely rebuffed.

Needles, yarn, and friends: What more do you need? Members of Columbia Sip & Knit knit by the waters of Lake Kittamaqundi in Columbia, Maryland. *Photograph by Alvaro J. Gonzalez*

In addition to bookstores, some other places that might host knitting groups include the following:

- **Libraries.** Two of my local libraries have knitting groups. The drawback is the expectation of being quiet, which is virtually impossible for my group. However, some libraries have separate meeting rooms where you are free to raise a ruckus.
- **Yarn shops.** Local yarn stores also will host knitting groups, and the best yarn stores often have a knitting group already in place. However, there may be an expectation that all knitting will be done with products purchased at the store, which can make things sticky for some knitters. On the other hand, if you purchase enough, you might be eligible for a discount!
- **Private residences.** If people are willing to open their homes and host a group, this could also work, but it's best for groups where everyone knows each other beforehand. My spinning guild occasionally has spinning sessions in members' homes, and the burden of hosting is eased by rotating who hosts the event.
- **Churches, community centers, and lodges.** These can also be good choices, since they are usually easy to find, may have excellent facilities, and are committed to community activities. My spinning guild has an arrangement with our town's community office and pays dreadfully low rent for the facility in exchange for the guild's participation in community events, which usually involve small children and fluffy wool. This allows the guild to do some interesting projects and workshops each year.
- **Anywhere.** The sky is the limit. Parks, bars, restaurants, or any venue where people gather on Earth is fair game. I do like to let the business know, so that

they can plan for the activity. There is also a growing movement called Stitch N' Pitch, where stitchers gather at the baseball parks to support their favorite major league teams. You *could* hold your knitting group on the space station if you could get everyone there, but all yarn would have to be in baggies attached to the knitters' respective belts to avoid snarls in zero gravity.

Go to the First Night—and Stay

Show up and stay for the duration. This sounds like a strange piece of advice, but consider that while our group meets from 6:00–9:00 p.m., members regularly roll in until 8:00 and sometimes stay later. In other words, don't get discouraged if you don't have a lively group in the first fifteen minutes.

Allow Everyone to Introduce Themselves

Go around and give everyone the opportunity to introduce themselves, explain their project, and talk about the yarn they're using. Let's face it, for knitters, chatting about yarn is the ultimate icebreaker.

Tell Everyone about It

I print business cards with the details of the knitting group to hand out when I see knitters on the street. Post meeting announcements online. Let The Knitting Guild Association know. Let the knitting teacher at your local craft store know. Shout it from the roof of the tallest building in the land. If your group outgrows your location, find a new one.

Beyond the Usual Meeting Time

As our group has grown, we have done a number of activities together, including touring our local yarn stores as a small group and attending nearby yarn shows, festivals, and classes. We also have the Lacis Museum of Lace and Textiles in our corner of the world, which we occasionally visit when an exhibit is of interest. There have even been occasions when some of us attended another knitting group on the weekend only to discover that everyone had the same idea! Once your group is established, here are some other things that you can do to make things interesting:

Yarn Crawls

Think pub or bar crawl, but with yarn. Meet outside of the normal knitting group night to crawl through the local or not-so-local yarn stores. Usually there is a meal involved, and possibly a drink or two. You need not buy anything, but the local yarn store owners will appreciate your patronage, especially when you ask them for help on a project later. There are occasionally more established yarn crawls sponsored by groups of the local yarn stores, with prizes and associated events. For my group, I usually keep it informal, set a date, and see who joins.

The following books and websites offer inspiration and aid in finding—or founding—a knitting community.

Knitter's Review

www.knittersreview.com

Knitter's Review is an online community started by Clara Parkes in 2001. It offers reviews of books, tools, and yarn, a fantastic calendar of knitting events around the country (*www.knittersreview.com/upcoming_events.asp*), members' forums, and more.

The Knitting Guild Association

www.tkga.com

The Knitting Guild Association (TKGA) was the first knitting guild founded in the United States. This is for serious knitters! Membership benefits include a subscription to *Cast On* magazine, free entry to Knit & Crochet Shows at TKGA conferences, and access to members-only online content, including free patterns, lessons, and master technique articles.

Knitting Guilds of Canada

www.canknit.com/guilds.html

This is a listing of Canadian knitting guilds on the Canadian Knitwear Designers & Artisans site. Most guilds meet regularly and welcome new members. There's even one that notes "boys welcome!"

Meetup

www.meetup.com

Meetup is a website that allows people with similar interests, such as knitting, to connect and arrange meetings. This is a great place to look for knitting groups in your area or to announce your own.

Lacis Museum of Lace and Textiles

www.lacis.com

The place for anyone interested in vintage, lace, or reenactment.

World Wide Knit in Public (WWKIP) Day

http://www.wwkipday.com/recent.htm

This site allows local knitting circles to post upcoming knit in public events they are hosting. It's also a great resource for knitters who are looking for knitting-related events in their area.

Knitalong: Celebrating the Tradition of Knitting Together by Larissa Brown and Martin John Brown, published by Stewart, Tabori & Chang, 2008

Stitch 'N Bitch Nation: 50 Hip, Even Funkier Patterns by Stitch 'N Bitch Designers Across America by Debbie Stoller, published by Workman, 2004

Festivals

In most knitting groups, someone always knows where and when the next knitting or fiber festival is planned, and someone else is always willing to go. Sometimes carpooling, hotel rooms, and bottles of wine are involved. Please do not drink and knit, as you may not recognize your project the next morning.

Charity Knitting

This can take many forms, such as everyone knitting a square for an afghan for Project Linus, baby hats to donate to the local hospital, or socks for soldiers. There are lots of ideas for charity knitting later in this book.

And Just About Anything Else You Can Dream Up

Recently, some members of my knitting group all went on a cruise to support another member who was in need of a little shakeup in her life. They all returned happy, tan, and with not a stitch knit. In this case, the members just agreed on a cruise they liked, but there are some established venues for knitting cruises, retreats, and similar events. Check with your local yarn shops, in knitting magazines, or online for these events.

This is the beauty of knitting groups: They will be there when you really need them. You just have to find (or found) them.

A Modern Knitter's Guide to Knitting Group Etiquette

by Kelley Dean-Crowley

My group has weathered more than five years of knitting together now, and that time has not been without its challenges. Over the years, we have defined some general etiquette for the knitting group. Think of etiquette as the tool that allows everyone to enjoy their time in the group.

Be Mindful of Your Host

If you are meeting in a coffee shop, bookstore, or some other place of business, please patronize them. We regularly buy tea at our host's café. You might periodically shop at the yarn store that hosts your group. Likewise, if there is something missing in the product mix of the store that hosts you, let them know so that they can accommodate the need.

Always Say Something Nice

Style is subjective. Although you may not care for the yarn, style, or design a fellow knitter has selected, don't tell her or him so. If you can't say anything nice, now is a good time to count your stitches or pull out that complex lace knitting project. It buys you some time to think of something positive to say, even if you can't imagine a use for a beer mug cozy knit in those particular colors of novelty yarn.

Help Each Other Out

If you see someone struggling with a skill or a project, lend a hand. And, when you're having trouble with a pattern, don't be shy about asking for help. However, don't abuse others' kindness; they are there to knit, too.

Respect Each Other's Beliefs

We have a knitter who is a leading member of a controversial local organization. On many occasions, the discussion has leaned toward the controversy, and we have all learned a lot. You simply never know where enrichment may come from. Without respect, there is no common ground upon which to build understanding.

No Creeps

If someone's behavior is making the group uncomfortable, politely ask her or him to leave, preferably in person, not via e-mail, snail mail, or carrier pigeon.

> **"Enjoy your knitting and the company and not necessarily in that order. After all, it's not every day that you can go to knitting group."**

"Unacceptable behavior" will vary from group to group, and it could be anything from expressing zero interest in actually knitting or crocheting, to hitting on married group members, to aggressively recruiting for the pyramid marketing scheme du jour. It's almost impossible for a group to know what it will be until they encounter it. Suffice it to say, if you're creeping the group out, you're out.

Enjoy Your Knitting and the Company
And not necessarily in that order. After all, it's not every day that you can go to knitting group.

Always Have an Extra Ball of Yarn and Set of Needles
You never know when someone will stop by without a project, or when you will need to teach someone's daughter or son who has tagged along.

Break the Rules on a Regular Basis
Always rely on your best judgment. Rules are just guidelines and are made to be broken.

Knit On
Need I say more?

Friendship Scarves

by Suzyn Jackson

Remember the friendship bracelets that you wore in junior high until they turned gray and disintegrated right off your wrist? This project uses the same concept: Each knitter knits her own scarf, while everyone shares yarn. It's a great way for a group of newbie knitters to learn their stuff, have fun, and take home something cool.

Start with a field trip to a yarn store. Each person buys a different color of super-bulky yarn. One or two striping or variegated yarns would add some extra interest. Make sure you all agree that the various colors look good together!

Then gather for knitting. Before you start, decide on a signal to pass the yarn. Every time a Beatles song plays on the oldies station? Every time a certain knitter (you know who) mentions her new boyfriend? Every time the cute waiter comes around to refresh your coffee?

Each person starts with the color she or he bought. At the signal, everyone breaks her yarn and passes her needles and scarf to the next person. It's like a drinking game, only instead of a headache, you get a cozy neck!

Number of Knitters

Three or more. Each knitter knits one scarf, but everyone shares yarn.

Finished Measurements

Width: Approximately 6 (12)"
Length: Whatever length you like

Materials

Yarn

Super-bulky yarn, a different color for each knitter. For this project, everyone should use the same brand and style of yarn. Each knitter should have enough yarn to make a good-sized scarf (decide ahead of time whether that means long and skinny or wide and bulky). The salesperson at the yarn store will be able to help you figure out how many balls you'll need. In the samples pictured, I used the following yarn:

- Lion Brand Wool-Ease Thick & Quick (80% acrylic/20% wool; 106 yds/170g per skein): Grass (131), Navy (110), and Cranberry (138)

Needles

Size 13 (9mm) or whatever size is recommended for your chosen yarn

Notions

Tapestry needle

Instructions

If you like long, skinny scarves, cast on 12 stitches. If you prefer wider scarves, cast on 24 stitches. The cast-on edge will look narrower than the final result; after a few rows, you will see just how wide your scarf will be.

Work in garter stitch (knit every row) until the "pass" signal.

Now, what you do next depends on the kind of person you are. If you just like to go with the flow, stop right where you are in the middle of a row. If you're fairly organized, work to the end of your row. And if anyone has ever called you a "neat freak," work to the end of the next wrong-side row (only the neat freaks have a right side and a wrong side in this pattern).

Cut your yarn, leaving a tail of 6–8". Hold on to your needles, and pass your ball of yarn. You don't always have to pass to the same person—mix it up! Start working with the new yarn, leaving a 6–8" tail as you begin. If you like, knot the tails loosely together (you'll need to unknot them eventually, so don't tie the knot too tightly).

Continue until everyone has used up her or his yarn. The quickest knitters can help the others use up their yarn.

When you are down to the last couple of yards of yarn, bind off (it's always better to have an extra yard of yarn than to run out halfway through your bind-off row—I know from experience!).

Undo all knots, then weave in all the loose ends using your tapestry needle.

Toss the scarf around your neck and enjoy the unique sensation of wearing something you made with your own hands. Think of it as a circle of knitting friends in portable form.

Give Your Scarves Away

Scarves make an excellent project for charitable giving. Contact your local shelters, hospitals, or places of worship to give within your own community or check out these organizations:

Red Scarf Project
www.orphan.org
The Orphan Foundation of America collects scarves to put in Valentine's Day care packages for college-bound foster youth.

Wool Works
www.woolworks.org/charity.html
A listing of charities that accept knitted donations, organized by state, from the Tuscaloosa (Alabama) Metro Animal Shelter to the Holy Spirit Knitting Ministry in Rock Springs, Wyoming.

Warm Woolies
www.warmwoolies.org
Warm Woolies is a nonprofit organization whose volunteers knit warm clothing for poverty-stricken children who would otherwise suffer from cold— and they supply the yarn! See their site for details.

Chapter Two
Connections Forged

Knitting circles bring people together in ways both expected and unexpected. The simple act of knitting together can foster an atmosphere of remarkable generosity and sharing. In this chapter, we explore the spirit of camaraderie that knitting together can create.

The patterns in this chapter range from the more intimate, where everyone works together to create a single garment, to the relatively casual sharing of odds and ends to produce gloriously varied hats. The harlequin purse can be knit solo, but since it uses a challenging technique and could have so many variations, it works well as a knitalong.

A Knitter's Tale

by Doug Brandt

I didn't even know a knitter until I was in graduate school in 1984. My house-mate, Ute, a skinny German woman with a blond flapper's hairdo and enor-mous blue Betty Boop eyes, arrived with drawers full of sweaters she'd made for herself: bulky sheep's wool and mohair concoctions striped in bright lemons, forest greens, and bubblegum pink. I didn't think much of her taste in colors, but I thought an awful lot of her.

I had a mad crush on Ute. I did everything to get her attention (short of tell-ing her about my crush), and I finally hit upon the notion of asking her to teach me how to knit. That certainly wasn't how the other guys were trying to get her attention (and they were). I thought that if we developed a strong student-teacher bond, maybe she'd fall for me.

So she taught me to knit. Out of a fat gray wool, I created a misshapen, hole-filled, garter stitch disaster that somehow, if only because of its length, almost resembled a scarf. Then she taught me to purl—all Continental style, of course—and we embarked on my first vest: heathered charcoal-gray with asymmetrical maroon stripes. It was unabashedly 1980s.

Ute dragged me to the yarn store and introduced me to the band of Little Old Ladies who sat there all day, knitting and gobbling. I slowly learned to knit, tightly and evenly, under Ute's patient hand, and I realized that I liked the feel of knitting. When the year ended and Ute flew back to Germany, our relationship remained at the level of teacher and student. (She actually once said to me, afterward, "You know, if we hadn't been housemates, something might have happened between us." Sigh.)

To my surprise, after she was gone, I realized that I needed to keep knitting. I was hooked and jonesing, and I knew where the yarn store was, and the gobbling ladies. The store was a wonderful little tax shelter owned by an elderly surgeon, who may well never have entered the store, and run by his wife, who, as her friends would confide to me, could "knit in about sixteen different languages, from British to Greek to Czech!"

Because the elderly women who knitted there were the only other knitters I knew, I would lug my knitting bag over to the shop after work and sit with them. (I'm a little embarrassed to admit that my knitting bag at that time was a goat skin. Or more precisely, a hollowed-out goat.) They helped me through my first white fisherman's sweater, knit with cables and bobbles and a fat shawl collar. I came to adore the ladies and got quite good at gobbling myself. Then I moved to Boston, and my knitting circle was suddenly gone.

Doug Brandt and his wife, Kathleen Keegan, knit at The Point Knitting Cafe in New York City. Doug is wearing his Alice Starmore Henry VIII sweater. *Photograph by Will Grega*

Just before I'd moved, I'd bought a quantity of Manos Del Uruguay skeins in purple and electric blue (still very 1980s), with the idea of making a blue sweater with vertical purple stripes, but I didn't have anyone to help me. I didn't know any yarn shops in Boston—or any knitters, for that matter. I didn't know how to design my own sweater, didn't know how to find a gauge or how to best measure myself, and I couldn't remember how to switch colors. I let my knitting get swallowed up in my busyness and pride. Moths got into my goat bag.

It wasn't until I moved to Providence, Rhode Island, with my wife-to-be, Kathy, in 1996 that the long-dormant yen to knit awoke in me. I'd been accepted into an acting program there, and I discovered a beautiful little yarn store called A Stitch Above, nestled in a quaint section of the posh East Side. The owner was young and hip and knew everything about yarns and knitting, and when I told her about the things I'd knitted in the past, she introduced me to the wondrous world of Alice Starmore.

I became a Starmore freak. My program was attached to a professional acting company, and whenever I was in one of the main-stage shows, I was usually playing small roles. With eight shows a week, I had lots of time to knit. I finished my first Starmore (Kittatinny, which Kathy still calls my Hamlet Sweater) my first year. That summer, I finished my second (St. Brigid, without the fringe) in Ohio while performing in *1776*. My third sweater was a cardigan (Grapevine, and it was for Kathy, a "groom's gift to the bride"). For my birthday that year, she bought me all of the yarn I'd need to make Starmore's Henry VIII, which would be my first Fair Isle.

But then we moved to New York, and my Starmore haven became just a comfortable memory. Despite the half-dozen or so decent yarn shops I found in Manhattan, I couldn't find a knitting circle, and I needed one. Yarn stores in New York City rarely had enough room for a table where folks could sit and gobble, and once again I locked my passion away in the closet with my stash. With the exception of that first hideous scarf, I'd pretty much stuck to stupidly hard and complicated projects—so I had skipped over a lot of extremely basic knitting skills (and my math skills are a tad embarrassing). I had no idea how I was going to make Henry VIII. I only knew Continental knitting, and I didn't understand stranding. That bag of twelve different gorgeous colors of Fair Isle wool lay untouched for nearly five years.

Then two things happened to rescue me and my neglected yarn. First, a yarn café opened up right by my house. The concept was novel but crucial. There I could order a soda or a latte and sit down for a little while and chat with other knitters—customers and staff. Simply being able to talk yarn and gauge and technique with other yarn heads was stimulating. I could relax. I could ask questions. (The opening of that first café coincided loosely with the onset of the knitting craze and the popularity of quick knits on giant needles with marvelously insane yarns.)

Second, in the elevator of my office building, I overheard a woman discussing a sweater she was making. I chimed in with something clever (I'm certain) that let her know I knew a little something about knitting, too. It turned out that we worked for different divisions of the same company, and she had organized a small knitting circle. She invited me to join, and I did. Most thrilling to me, she was a Starmore freak, and she owned every book Ms. Alice has ever published—down to those fat pamphlets from the old Tomato Factory. Kristen had even taken a class from Ms. Alice—and had been chewed out by her, which I would have considered quite an honor.

The circle met weekly in our company's little kitchen, growing and shrinking according to other folks' schedules and insecurities, but Kristen and I were the serious ones—making sure to meet as regularly as our schedules allowed. Then the second yarn café opened up in the city, right on the train line that ran past our building.

Kristen had learned to knit, as I had, Continental style (and from a German), but she had also taught herself British style so she could work with the others in the circle. She taught me the British style, and I began to work on the two-color stranding necessary for making Henry VIII—or Henry, as he became known over the year it took me to knit him. Kristen also stood with me as I cut the steeks at Henry's armholes and neck, the most frightening thing I'd ever done as a knitter. (Don't ever believe all the books that tell you your steeks won't unravel. All of mine began to, and I had to tack them down with yarn before I picked up stitches for the sleeves and neck. But I digress.)

Eventually, the others in our circle either left the company or lost interest in knitting, but Kristen and I have hung together, making time whenever we can. We head down to The Point, a yarn café in Manhattan and my favorite yarn shop in the city, where we knit, drink cream sodas, and gobble with the customers and the staff. As the knitting craze has died down a little to reveal a generation of women and men who really got hooked—and are knocking off complicated lacework and serious designs like they're nothing—my tight little community of two has grown into a network of dozens, even hundreds. (Most convenient for me, the Internet has become an additional resource when my questions are so basic that I'm embarrassed to ask a live human.)

Knowing—even slightly—a lot of people in this community makes it possible for me to knit. Kristen and I really don't constitute a knitting circle, per se; two points form more of a line than a circle. But I'm not confident enough to make it completely on my own, and this loose connection to many like-minded folks in the yarn cafés and online keeps me knitting. It also makes this city of eight million people feel much smaller and more manageable than it would otherwise be. I meet knitters in coffee shops, on the train, on the bus. One of my favorite New York moments occurred one evening after work. I was sitting alone in a Starbucks, working away at Henry. A woman who'd been sitting next to me for about a half-hour leaned over and said, "Excuse me. Is that Henry VIII?" It turned out that she knew all of Alice Starmore's patterns by name—despite never having tackled one. We chatted for a time, and I said, "You look familiar to me. Have we ever met?"

And she said, "I think you spoke to me once, when I was knitting on the subway."

My knitting circle has become more of a knitting net; it has caught me a hundred times and carried me farther than I ever could have gone on my own. I can't knit in a vacuum, and I will never have to again.

" My knitting circle has become more of a knitting net; it has caught me a hundred times and carried me farther than I ever could have gone on my own. I can't knit in a vacuum, and I will never have to again. "

Harlequin Purse

Design by Suzyn Jackson

What do you need to take on a challenge? Some people need a supportive environment with plenty of help along the way, while others thrive on competition. If several people take on this entrelac purse, you'll get plenty of both types of encouragement. It's a purse party!

Entrelac looks a lot harder than it is. The trickiest parts of this technique are working the short rows for the base triangles and picking up stitches along the side edges. Easy as it is, the results look like magic: a "woven" fabric of knitted strips—or so it seems.

Number of Knitters
One or more. Each knitter knits her own purse and lends moral support to the others.

Finished Measurements
Width: Approx 13$\frac{1}{2}$"
Depth: Approx 6$\frac{1}{2}$"
Actual size of your purse will be smaller or larger, depending on your choice of yarn.

Materials
Yarn
One or two colors of any yarn you like. Two balls of each color should be plenty for most yarns. I recommend a smooth, stretchy yarn, as you'll need to be able to see your stitches clearly in order to pick them up easily. Color A should be your darker color, and Color B your lighter color.
In the sample pictured, I used a worsted weight yarn, some old Reynolds Coco II (50% wool/50% rayon; 136 yds/100g per skein) from my mother's stash.

Needles
24-inch circular needle one or two sizes smaller than called for on the yarn label or whatever gives you a firm gauge

Notions
Tapestry needle, stitch markers

Gauge
Gauge depends on the yarn you choose to work with; you should strive for a nice, firm fabric at a gauge that is somewhat denser than that given on the yarn label.
For the sample pictured, 20 sts and 28 rows = 4" (10cm) in St st.

Pattern Notes

Entrelac looks a lot more complicated than it is, but the only skills needed are knitting, purling, picking up stitches, and working decreases. You'll also be working short rows for the base triangles, but they're no more than knitting, purling, and turning. Follow the diagram while reading the explanation that follows.

After casting on, you'll start by making a base layer of triangles. The triangles are worked one at a time, back and forth, adding 1 new stitch to each triangle every WS row until the triangle is complete. The triangles "lean" to the right.

Next, you'll pick up and knit stitches along the side of 1 triangle and work a rectangle that "leans" to the left, attaching the top of the rectangle to the side of the adjacent triangle by working an ssk decrease; you'll repeat this until you have created a layer of left-leaning rectangles across the top of the triangles.

For the next layer, you'll work right-leaning rectangles by picking up and purling stitches along one side of a rectangle on the previous layer and attach the top of the rectangle to the side of the adjacent rectangle by working a p2tog decrease; you'll repeat this until you have created a layer of right-leaning rectangles across the top of the first layer of rectangles.

This purse is knitted in the round, eliminating the "side triangles" that you'll see in entrelac patterns that are worked flat. The bottom is a straight seam (which practically disappears when you sew it), making a clever "envelope" shape, which is then gathered at the top.

Instructions
First Layer (Base Triangles)
Using A and circular needle, CO 97 sts; turn.

Sl 1 st from right needle to left needle. Place a stitch marker on the right needle for beg of rnd, and join, taking care not to twist sts.

First Triangle
Row 1 (WS): P2tog to join first and last cast-on sts, p1, turn—96 sts.
Row 2 (RS): K2, turn.
Row 3: P3, turn.
Row 4: K3, turn.
Row 5: P4, turn.
Row 6: K4, turn.
Continue in this manner, adding 1 purl stitch every WS row and knitting back to the stitch marker on the following RS row, until you purl 12 (12 stitches on right needle to the left of the stitch marker). You should have one triangle hanging from your needle. Do not turn. Place another stitch marker on the right needle.

Second and All Other Triangles
Row 1 (WS): P2, turn.
Row 2 (RS): K2, turn.
Complete as for First Triangle.
Rep Second Triangle until you have 8 triangles and are back to the first stitch marker.
Cut A, leaving enough yarn to sew in later.

Second Layer (Left-Leaning Rectangles)
With RS facing and using B, pick up and knit 12 sts along the side edge of the first triangle, turn.
Row 1 (WS): P12, turn.
Row 2 (RS): K11, ssk (working the last st of the rectangle together with the first st of the last triangle), turn.

Rep Rows 1 and 2 until you have joined all the stitches of the last triangle to the rectangle.
Begin the next rectangle by picking up and knitting stitches along the next triangle. (Be careful on the first purl row not to work any stitches from the previous rectangle.) Finish as for the first rectangle.

Repeat until you have 8 rectangles worked in B. Cut B, leaving enough yarn to sew in later.

Third Layer (Right-Leaning Rectangles)

With WS facing and using A, pick up and purl 12 sts along the side edge of the first left-leaning rectangle.

Row 1 (RS): K12, turn.

Row 2 (WS): P11, p2tog (working the last st of the rectangle together with the first st of the left-leaning rectangle below), turn.

Rep Rows 1 and 2 until you have joined all the stitches of the left-leaning rectangle to the right-leaning rectangle.

Begin the next rectangle by picking up and knitting stitches along the next left-leaning rectangle. (Be careful on the first purl row not to work any stitches from the previous rectangle.) Finish as for the first rectangle.

Repeat until you have 8 rectangles worked in A.

Cut A, leaving enough yarn to sew in later.

Final Layer (Left-Leaning Rectangles with Eyelets)

Work as for the Second Layer (right-leaning rectangles) until there are 3 sts remaining in the right-leaning rectangle that you are joining.

RS: K2, k2tog, [yo] twice, ssk, k5, ssk, turn.

WS: P9, purl into front and back of the double yo, p2, turn.

Work next 2 rows as usual—there will be 1 st remaining in the right-leaning rectangle that you are joining.

RS: BO 10 sts, ssk, BO 1 st, leaving 1 st on right needle.

Pick up and knit 12 sts for next rectangle, binding off the last st of previous rectangle over the first picked-up st.

Work the eyelets when there are 3 stitches remaining in the right-leaning rectangle that you are joining.
Photograph by Alvaro J. Gonzalez

Repeat until you have worked and bound off all 8 rectangles.

Finishing
I-Cord Ties
(Make 2)

With A, cast on 4 sts. Do not turn.

*Slip the sts back to left-hand needle and k4, do not turn; rep from * until cord measures 24" or desired length of handles.

Lay purse flat and match up 4 triangles on either side. Sew the triangles together to form bottom seam.

Lay the purse flat again, and give it a tiny twist so that none of the top rectangles are folded. On one side of purse, fold the tops of the first two rectangles together so that the wrong sides are facing each other. Repeat with the other two rectangles on that side. Thread one length of I-cord through the 4 holes, then sew the ends of the I-cord together. Repeat on other side of purse.

Weave in all ends.

Variations

You can easily create a tote-sized version of this bag by increasing the original cast-on count by multiples of 24 stitches (each multiple of 24 stitches makes two additional rectangles in each layer) and by repeating the second and third layers of rectangles as many times as you like.

The two-color scheme increases the illusion of a woven fabric, but there's nothing to say you couldn't make every layer—or every rectangle!—a different color.

The rectangles in this pattern are basic stockinette stitch. Add a cable or a bit of intarsia if you are so inclined.

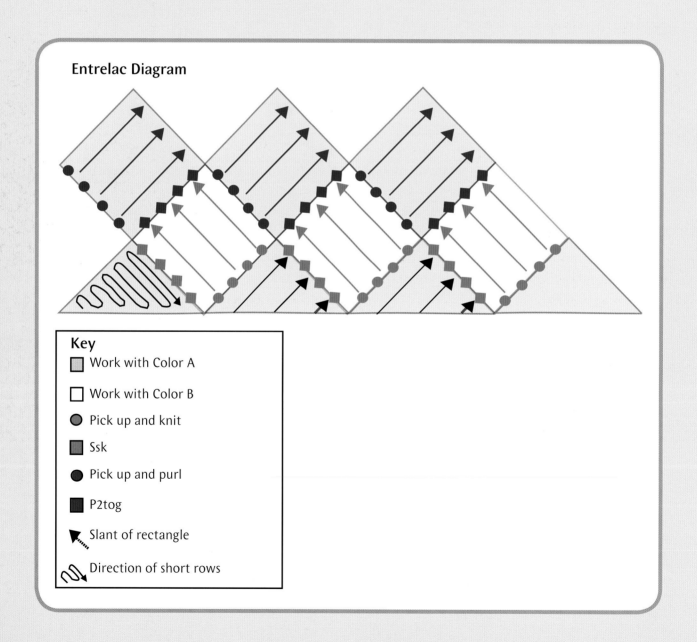

Entrelac Diagram

Key

- ▦ Work with Color A
- ☐ Work with Color B
- ⬤ Pick up and knit
- ▦ Ssk
- ⬤ Pick up and purl
- ▪ P2tog
- ▼ Slant of rectangle
- ∿ Direction of short rows

My Friend's Song

by Sue Hawley

I knit hats
in bright bombastic colors:
purples and pinks,
orange red:
huge zinnias for your head—
noisy and funny.

My friend chose colors for hers:
dollskin pink,
beige of ancient lace,
then the vague blue of the sky on a humid day,
finally—rust like the oak leaf
late on the tree.

I cast on the pink,
knitted quietly,
then felt myself waiting—
hanging, dangling.
I added beige next—
itchy—"Where's the noise?
Bring on the clowns."

Then the vague blue,
and I heard a little hum.
I knitted on, added a speck of rust.
The hum made a quiet song.
I repeated a bit of beige,
and heard myself humming
my friend's tune.

For Rosemary—Fall 1993

Whether they help you learn a new skill or suggest a new color combination, friends can expand your knitting world in wondrous ways. *Photograph by Alvaro J. Gonzalez*

Editor's note: This poem was written for my mother, Rosemary Jackson. She and Sue Hawley were both members of the Women's Spirituality Group of Grace Church in Amherst, Massachusetts, which inspired the pattern that follows. Sue and Rosemary knit many hats together over long talks that ranged from the role of women in the church to the role of pink in a color scheme.

Odds and Ends Hats

Design by Suzyn Jackson

It's very rare that the final stitches of any project use up the final yards of yarn. More often, you have anywhere from several yards to most of a ball left over. It's never quite enough for another project, but it pains many knitters to throw it out. So what do you do with it?

The Women's Spirituality Group of Grace Church in Amherst, Massachusetts, came up with a solution. Whenever someone finished a knitting project, she would toss her leftover yarn into a bin that was kept at the church. Anyone was welcome to sift through the bin for yarn, pulling out combinations of textures and colors that pleased her. The knitters made hats with the odds and ends and sold them at the annual St. Nicholas fair. The fair opened at 9:00 a.m., and the hats were usually sold out by 10:00. All proceeds went to the church.

This system could easily be replicated by any knitting group. Sell the hats, donate them to a local shelter, or keep them and wear them!

Number of Knitters
Three or more. Each knitter knits one or more hats, but everyone shares yarn.

Finished Measurements
As desired by knitter

Materials
Yarn
Collected odds and ends. If you're using yarns with vastly different gauges, stick to one size of yarn for most of the hat, and work narrow (one- to two-row) stripes with the thicker/thinner yarn. Often, thinner yarns can be doubled to approximate the gauge of thicker yarns.

Needles
Experiment by swatching the main yarn for the hat with various-sized needles until you come up with a fabric weight that you like, then use those needles for the hat. The hats can be knitted flat on straight needles (my preferred method) or in the round. If you like to knit in the round, you can start on circular needles, but you'll need to switch to double-pointed needles for the top of the crown.

Notions
Tapestry needle

Gauge
It's important to measure your gauge for the most prominent yarn so that you can figure out how many stitches to cast on. Once you have decided on yarn and needles, do a standard gauge swatch to determine the number of stitches per inch.

Pattern Notes

Before you begin, you'll need to calculate 3 numbers (total cast-on stitch count, number of "slices," and number X) using the worksheet below.

Gauge (sts/inch):_____

Hat circumference: _____

Cast on: _____ Adjusted: _____Plus 2 edge sts, if working flat: _____

Slices: _____

Stitches per slice: _____

Number X: _____

Cast-On Number

Standard head circumferences are

- Baby: 14"
- Toddler: 16"
- Child: 18"
- Adult: 20–22"

Or, you can just measure your own head and make the hat fit yourself! Multiply your preferred circumference by your gauge-per-inch to determine the number of stitches to cast on. To make your hat snug, make it 1 or 2 inches *smaller* than your head size.

Number of Slices

The top shaping for a simple knit hat looks like a pie that has been cut. Once you have determined how many stitches you'll need to cast on for the size of hat you are knitting, you need to figure out how many slices of pie you'll have. (When shaping the top, you'll be working decreases to form the "cuts" in the pie.)

Here are basic guidelines:

- 36–72 sts = 6 slices
- 64–96 sts = 8 slices
- 80–120 sts = 10 slices
- 120+ sts = 12 slices

Notice that there's some overlap in these numbers. Use fewer slices to make a pointier hat, more to make a rounder hat. You can also have an odd number of slices, if that works out better for you.

Number of Stitches per Slice

Now you need to figure out how many stitches you'll have in each slice for the first row of slices. Divide your cast-on number by your slices number. Is it a whole number? If yes, you're done. If not, you should adjust your cast-on number until your slices number divides evenly into it.

Slice Diagram

Example:
Gauge: 4 sts = 1"
Head size: 21"
Cast on: 84 sts [4 x 21]
Slices: 8
Stitches per slice: Adjust cast-on count to 80 sts, so 10 sts per slice

Number X

Now subtract 2 from your stitches-per-slice number. This is number X.

One last thing: If you plan to knit the hat flat (as opposed to in the round), add 2 stitches to your cast-on number; these stitches are your "edge stitches" and will disappear when you sew the seam.

Instructions
Cuff

Cast on the number of stitches you figured in the Pattern Notes section. If you want a ribbed cuff, work in K1, P1 rib for a while—this will keep the hat snug over cold ears. For an extra-snug cuff, use needles one to two sizes smaller than you used for your gauge swatch. If you want a rolled cuff, work in stockinette stitch immediately—this will result in a looser fit. Stick to one color for your rib or roll, then work in stripes or any other pattern you like, using a variety of yarns.

Work until the piece, rolled or cuffed as you please, reaches from the top of your ear to the top of your head (the top shaping will give you enough extra space to cover your ears). This could be anywhere from 5–12".

Top Shaping

Note: These instructions are written assuming that you are knitting flat. If you are knitting in the round, change all purl stitches to knit stitches and switch to double-pointed needles when the stitches no longer fit comfortably on your circular needle. You'll also need to eliminate the edge st instructions.

Row 1 (RS): K1 (edge st), *knit [X] sts, k2tog; rep from * to last st, k1 (edge st).

Row 2 (WS): Purl.

Row 3: K1, *knit [X - 1] sts, k2tog; rep from * to last st, k1.

Row 4: Purl.

Continue in this way, knitting one stitch fewer between k2togs on each RS row, until you have worked the row/round with 5 sts between k2togs.

If working flat:

Next row (WS): P1, *p2tog, p4; rep from * to last st, p1.

Next row (RS): K1, *k3, k2tog; rep from * to last st, k1.

Next row: P1, *p2tog, p2; rep from * to last st, p1.

Next row: K1, *k1, k2tog; rep from * to last st, k1.

Next row: P2tog across row.

If working in the round:

Work 1 stitch fewer between k2togs every round; on last round, k2tog around.

Finishing

Cut yarn, leaving a tail long enough to sew side seam. Using a tapestry needle, draw yarn through the remaining stitches on needle. Sew side seam. Sew in all loose ends. Block as necessary.

Hats for Charity

Many charities accept hats. Here are just a few to get you started. Please review the requirements of each charity before you start knitting for them.

Caps for a Cure
http://groups.yahoo.com/group/capsforacure
An online knitalong group that knits caps for chemotherapy patients.

ChemoCaps
www.chemocaps.com
Free patterns and encouragement for knitters to donate caps to their local cancer treatment center.

Hats 4 the Homeless
www.hats4thehomeless.org
This charity accepts store-bought and handmade hats. They are then distributed at St. Francis Xavier's Soup Kitchen on West 15th Street in New York City on the weekend before Christmas.

Knitting for Noggins
www.archildrens.org/volunteer/Knitting_for_Noggins.asp
Help make a difference in the lives of patients and families at Arkansas Children's Hospital.

My Bubbie, My Barbie

by Meira Drazin

My Bubbie, my father's mother, has never been an easy woman to get along with. Maybe it was the Holocaust, maybe it was the rest of her life: the disappointments, the poverty, the ill-suited marriage, the illnesses as a direct result of extreme deprivation in the camps as a teenager. She is bitter and can find a creative way to put anybody down. She's also an avid reader in English, even though she only learned the language in her twenties. In a rare gesture when I was maybe eleven or twelve, she lent me her copy of Herman Wouk's *Marjorie Morningstar*. I read it again last year, and I had the strangest feeling of déjà vu in a story I vaguely recalled, like something just on the tip of my tongue, as the plot filled out and the nuances, sexual and otherwise, took form.

As with *Marjorie Morningstar*, when I picked up knitting again as an adult, I found shades of gray and sophistication, truths and longings, disappointment, sadness, and satisfaction in ways I could have only felt obliquely as a child.

When I was eight or nine, my grandmother taught me how to knit. We used a maroon wool from a leftover skein, and I made a scarf for my Barbies using only the knit stitch. She did the tassels. That was the first and last item I knitted for many years, and I don't remember the actual learning process, but I do remember that scarf. For a long time, it was a prominent accessory featured in all my Barbie

The author's grandmother, 2008. *Photograph by Meira Drazin*

story lines—it worked especially well as a shawl for *Little House on the Prairie* stories, as well as for the shtetl episodes where Barbie was called "Raizel."

I will blushingly admit that I probably played Barbies a little too long, well into junior high at least. But growing up in a modern Orthodox home on those long Shabbat afternoons of no TV and no possibility of driving to a friend's house, sick of bossing around my younger brothers, I either played Barbies or read.

After that wool scarf for Barbie, though, I never had another knitting lesson with my Bubbie. I don't know why. Perhaps she saw it as nothing more than an isolated activity one afternoon while I was visiting, and not a skill or a passion to pass on to her granddaughter. Maybe she thought I wasn't interested. Maybe there just weren't that many afternoons that we spent together. But I didn't hold knitting needles again until I was in my twenties.

I finished grad school in the spring of 2000 and got married at the end of the summer. I landed my dream job at a magazine in Manhattan, but, being a Canadian, I had to wait for my visa to come through before I could start working. By November I was starting to go out of my mind: I was dependent on my husband for money; even worse, I was bored to the point of depression. Every night I would try to have a plan for the next day, but even after a leisurely breakfast, a spinning class at the gym, a drawn-out lunch over the *The New York Times*, and perhaps a museum, there were still several hours to be filled before I could pounce on my husband as soon as he walked in the door. I am not exaggerating when I say that walking into a well-known yarn shop on the Upper West Side for the first time was like falling into a magical place that gave substance and meaning to my amorphous existence.

> **"Every day I would go to the shop and sit and knit with the other women. There were regulars, there were those who popped in to start a new project and needed to do a gauge, there were those who needed help or advice (knitting or otherwise), and there were the store owners and assistants."**

I opened the door on a blustery late fall day, climbed the old carpeted stairs to the second-floor shop, and felt a blast of warm air along with the chatter of women of all ages sitting around a table, knitting. Somebody had time to cast some stitches onto a needle for me, and it was like riding a bicycle. Then they showed me how to purl, and I was off. "Okay, you can make a sweater now," one of the shop owners said. We picked out a hunter green yarn as thick as my finger and size 16 needles. She printed out a pattern for me and told me to come back when I got to the shaping for the arms. I came back the next day. The sweater was finished by the end of the week.

Every day I would go to the shop and sit and knit with the other women. There were regulars, there were those who popped in to start a new project and needed to do a gauge, there were those who needed help or advice (knitting or otherwise), and there were the store owners and assistants. As anyone who's spent some time in yarn shops knows, after an hour of sitting at the table knitting, everyone knows way too much about each other—collectively up in arms about the daughter-in-law who was a bully or the husband who never came home or the boyfriend who bought a new bed without getting his girlfriend's opinion. I don't remember what I talked about. But I tried on the feeling of camaraderie, of women who, for whatever reason, had made the time or were using this to fill the time, and it fit.

I finally began working full-time, but the knitting obsession continued. When I came to visit in Toronto, I would take whatever I was knitting over to my grandmother's to show her. As I had already discovered at the yarn store, knitting is a key that unlocks conversation, or at least chatter. It turned out knitting was a way to talk to my Bubbie, to avoid potential landmines, and to connect to her in a way we hadn't been able to since the days of Barbie and *Marjorie Morningstar*.

When I was growing up, topics before the war were off limits—or perhaps, haunted by the stories in the books I was reading, I was simply too afraid to bring them up. Only since I started bringing my knitting over did I find out that my grandmother was one of four children. And that she was one of a very small quota of Jews accepted to an exclusive teacher's college. She was crystal-sharp about the past and less so about the present. On one of my visits, we sat drinking tea at the kitchen table, linoleum underfoot, teal oven in the background. She told me that her mother owned what she termed a "dress salon" in Czechoslovakia.

"Oh, so you learned to sew and knit from her?"

"No—I only learned once I got to Toronto."

She was the first cousin of my grandfather's first wife, who had perished with their five children in Auschwitz. As the only surviving members of their families, they decided to marry. In 1950, they escaped Czechoslovakia with my aunt, then three years old, and eventually they made it to Toronto, where my father was born. There, in a one-bedroom flat where the neighbors all shared one lavatory, my grandmother saw a picture of a belted sweater coat that she wanted my aunt to have, and she decided to try to make it herself.

Later on, on another visit, I found out that, actually, she had learned to knit as a child (although not from her mother, whom she described as "a crocheter, not a knitter"). But what she meant was that it wasn't until she was a survivor, an immigrant in a new country with a new life, that her love of creating really took shape. I realized that, as for me, rediscovering knitting helped her bridge a gap in her adult life, and it opened a door to a passion filled with nuance and meaning—a passion that has endured even her inability to vanquish fingers that are too gnarled to hold her needles anymore.

Over the years, she saved hundreds of dollars, making for her and her family what she could not afford to buy off the rack. Buying discontinued colors, copying designs, staying up at the kitchen table until all hours of the morning to finish a hem so that it lay perfectly. There was nothing my grandmother couldn't make. And everything with a flair, a little shot of pizzazz—a cap, a cape, a crocheted flower to sit jauntily on a beret. Her closets are filled with a wardrobe of suits she knitted herself, what I thought of as her uniform when I was a child—the skirts fully lined, each jacket expertly fitted with shoulder pads. She rarely gets dressed anymore, but her foam wig heads still sport the matching hats.

Of course, it wasn't just saving money, it was the thrill of the project. The excitement of an idea coming to fruition. Of seeing the design literally take shape. Of ripping out and starting again until it was just right.

"It's a lot of work," my Bubbie said once, fingering the back of a cardigan where I had finally reached the point I could start shaping for the raglan inset. "And when it's finished, you don't see the one stitch after another, how long it takes to grow. But when you are finished, you are so proud of your accomplishment."

Indeed, I know that catch, that slight sticking out of my chest while trying to keep my voice neutral when someone compliments that sweater my daughter is wearing, and I admit I made it myself.

But there is only one thing I can ever remember my grandmother making for me. We planned it together: a tiered maroon skirt and matching vest. The vest was probably a better idea in theory than in practice—what eleven-year-old would wear a matching knitted outfit? I know I did wear the skirt for a while. I wish I had worn it more. And now that I think about it, it was made with that same maroon wool as the one used to knit the scarf for my Barbies.

> "I realized that, as for me, rediscovering knitting helped her bridge a gap in her adult life, and it opened a door to a passion filled with nuance and meaning—a passion that has endured even her inability to vanquish fingers that are too gnarled to hold her needles anymore."

Striped Kimono

Design by Suzyn Jackson

This unusual sweater makes for an ambitious and spectacular group project. Entirely made of "strips" of knitting, there is no shaping. The result is a stunning sweater that uses only novice-level knitting skills. When planning, remember that the seams take almost as long as the knitting!

This sweater could be a warm hug to a group member who's ill, a special memento for a member who's moving away, or a group charity project. Because it is so easy to customize the fit, you could even make a version for each member of your knitting circle, each in her favorite colors.

Number of Knitters

Three to eighteen. Each knitter knits one or more strips.

Sizes

Small (Large)

Finished Measurements

Chest: 38 (46)"

Length: 22 (24)"

Shoulder width: 19"

Sleeve length: 13–15", depending on edging style

Sleeve circumference: 20 (24)"

The measurements of this garment are easily adjustable—see diagram for details.

Materials
Yarn

Whatever yarn you like. The pattern is most effective when stripes contrast in either color or texture, so don't all use the same yarn. The yarns used in the sample are

- Lion Brand Homespun (98% acrylic/2% polyester; 185 yds/170g per skein): 2 skeins Olive #378
- Patons Classic Wool (100% merino wool; 223 yds/100g per skein): 1 skein Leaf Green #240
- Lion Brand Lion Suede (100% polyester; 122 yds/85g per skein): 1 skein Olive #132
- Lion Brand Jiffy (100% acrylic; 135 yds/85g per skein): 1 skein Grass Green #173
- Lion Brand Wool-Ease (80% acrylic/20% wool; 197 yds/85g per skein): 1 skein Grass #131
- Moda Dea Caché (75% wool/22% acrylic/3% polyester; 72 yds/50g per skein): 1 skein Smartie #2765

Needles

Whatever needle sizes are necessary to create an agreeable fabric with each yarn. It is not necessary to use the same needle size for all strips.

Notions

A few tapestry needles (to share the work of seaming)

Gauge

Swatch to determine gauge; each yarn and stitch pattern may be a different gauge.

Special Technique

4-st I-Cord: Cast on 4 sts. K4. *Do not turn, slip stitches back to left-hand needle and k4; rep from * until cord is desired length. Bind off.

Nonrolling Pattern Stitches

Garter Stitch (any number of stitches)
Knit all rows.

Seed Stitch (any number of stitches)
Row 1 (RS): K1, *p1, k1; rep from * to end of row.
Row 2: Knit the purl stitches and purl the knit stitches.
Rep Row 2 for pat.

Double Moss Stitch (multiple of 4 sts)
Rows 1 and 2: *K2, p2; rep from * across.
Rows 3 and 4: *P2, k2; rep from * across.
Rep Rows 1–4 for pat.

Pattern Notes

The sample kimono was made with the bottom and front borders in St st and I-cord edging all around. Other possible borders (shown in gray and blue on diagram) are suggested under Variations.

See suggestions for adjusting the finished measurements under Variations, below.

Instructions

Before you begin, lay out clippings of the yarns you intend to use on the diagram to make sure that you like the arrangement, balance, and juxtapositions. If using yarns of varying weights, try to keep the thicker yarns toward the middle of the garment so that heavier strips don't pull lighter ones out of shape. You will need to swatch all yarns and your chosen stitch patterns for gauge so that you can figure out how many stitches to cast on. Remember to add a one-stitch "seam allowance" on both sides of each strip.

All the pieces are long strips. For the sample, we cast on the number of stitches for the short side, and worked until the length matched the long side. You could work the strips in the other direction as well: cast on the number of stitches for the long side, then work until the length matches the short side. Or, combine the two techniques—you are the master of your knitting!

If working I-cord edging, using any yarn and any stitch, knit the following:

2 pieces 2" x 20"
4 pieces 3" x 20"
2 pieces 4" x 20"
*2 (4) pieces 2" x 36 (40)"
2 pieces 3" x 36 (40)"
*1 piece 4" x 33 (41)" [see below]
1 piece 5" x 18 (20)"
Size large only: 2 pieces 4" x 22"

If not working I-cord edging, using any yarn and a *nonrolling* stitch, knit the following border pieces:

2 pieces 3" x 20 (24)" for sleeve border
*2 pieces 2" x 36 (40)" [*replaces the 2 of the "any stitch" pieces 2" x 36 (40)" above]
*1 piece 4" x 33 (41)" [*replaces the 4" x 33 (41)" "any stitch" piece above]

Finishing

Block all pieces to appropriate measurements. Refer to the diagram for placement and assembly of the sweater. Because there are so many seams, share the work of sewing everything together. Sew the seams in the following order (refer to the Seams section on page 134):

Size Small

First, sew all the body and sleeve strips together. Then sew the ends of the sleeve strips together to form the underarm seam. Continue that seam along the side edges of the outermost main body strips. Finally, sew the longest strip around the hem.

Size Large

First, sew all the body and sleeve strips together. Sew the cuff ends together. Sew the gusset from the cuff to the hem, along the ends of the sleeve strips and the side edges of the outermost main body strips. Finally, sew the longest strip around the hem.

I-Cord Edging

After the sweater has been blocked and assembled, knit 4-st I-cords as follows:

- 1 approx 82 (94)" long, to go from center back of neck down the front, around the waist, and back up to the center back of neck again. Do not cut the yarn until you are almost done sewing on the I-cord, just in case you need to make it longer.
- 2 approx 20 (24)" long, 1 to go around the edge of each sleeve. Do not cut the yarn until you are almost done sewing on the I-cord, just in case you need to make it longer.

Sew on I-cord edging using mattress stitch (see Seams—pull apart two rows of the I-cord to see the "bars.")

Variations

To increase sleeve length: Add strips to the sleeves.

To increase chest size and shoulder width: Add strips to the main body.

To increase chest size without increasing shoulder width:
- Size small: Add a gusset and make the cuffs longer by the width of the gusset
- Size large: Make the gusset wider and the cuffs longer.

To increase the length: Make the central strips and gussets longer. The middle back strip should be half the length of the other body strips.

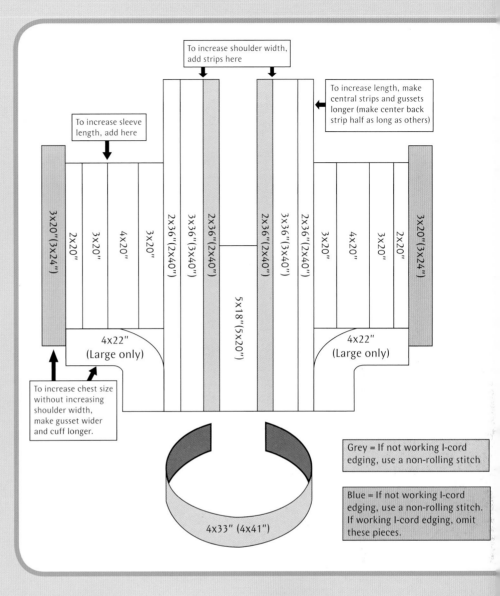

To increase shoulder width, add strips here

To increase length, make central strips and gussets longer (make center back strip half as long as others)

To increase sleeve length, add here

3x20"(3x24")

2x20"

3x20"

4x20"

3x20"

2x36"(2x40")

3x36"(3x40")

2x36"(2x40")

5x18"(5x20")

2x36"(2x40")

3x36"(3x40")

2x36"(2x40")

3x20"

4x20"

3x20"

2x20"

3x20"(3x24")

4x22" (Large only)

4x22" (Large only)

To increase chest size without increasing shoulder width, make gusset wider and cuff longer.

4x33" (4x41")

Grey = If not working I-cord edging, use a non-rolling stitch

Blue = If not working I-cord edging, use a non-rolling stitch. If working I-cord edging, omit these pieces.

New Skills Blanket

Design by Suzyn Jackson

In her essay "The Baby Blue Blankie" in *Knitting Yarns and Spinning Tales*, Kay Dorn wrote of knitting lacy blankets for each of her grandchildren. She chose lace because she "knew how babies love to push their fingers through the holes when they rub the cuddly yarn under their noses."

I had never thought of a lacy baby blanket before I read Ms. Dorn's essay, but it makes perfect sense. Babies first learn about the world through touch, whether it's the soft caress of Mother's hands or the intriguing holes in a blanket.

I translated this idea into a group project—with a twist. We start from the classic group afghan: Everybody knits a square. Here's the twist: To honor the new life that this blanket will wrap up, each knitter learns a new pattern—one with lots of texture for Baby's amusement, of course. Lace, cables, bobbles, and entrelac are all appropriate. A novice might try out a seed or basket stitch. Of course, the ultimate "new skill" is learning to knit in the first place, so a garter-stitch square from someone who has never knit would be absolutely appropriate.

Planning this project can be a lot of fun. Pull out a stitch dictionary (see the Sources of Inspiration sidebar for my favorites), and soon everyone will be reminiscing about that sweater they abandoned in college, or how nicely this texture would knit up for socks. Shy souls can pick a pattern that a buddy has mastered so that help is near. More adventurous knitters can strike out on a new path.

Sources of Inspiration

The Encyclopedia of Knitting: A Step–by–Step Visual Guide, with an Inspirational Gallery of Finished Works
by Lesley Stanfield and Melody Griffiths, published by Running Press, 2000
This beautifully illustrated guide to knitting stitches has both basic and advanced patterns. This is the book I used to teach myself new skills for the illustrated blanket.

A Treasury of Knitting Patterns
by Barbara G. Walker, published by Schoolhouse Press, 1998
This series (there are four books) is prized by many knitters as the most complete resource of knitting patterns.

The Harmony Guides: Knit & Purl: 250 Stitches to Knit; Cables & Arans: 250 Stitches to Knit; Lace & Eyelets: 250 Stitches to Knit; by Erika Knight (Editor), published by Interweave Press

Vogue Knitting Stitchionary Volume One: Knit & Purl: The Ultimate Stitch Dictionary from the Editors of Vogue Knitting Magazine
by Trisha Malcolm (Editor), published by Sixth&Spring Books, 2005
This volume and its follow-ups, *Volume Two: Cables* and *Volume Three: Color Knitting* cover a wide spectrum of stitches.

Number of Knitters

Two to thirteen for the small blanket, two to twenty-one for the large one. Each knitter knits one or more pieces of the blanket.

Finished Measurements

24" x 30" (30" x 39") before border is added

Materials

Yarn

Most baby yarn is soft, fine acrylic that is perfect for this project. Traditionally, it comes in soft pastels—what some people (okay, me) might call "namby-pamby colors." You can use any yarn for this project—any gauge, any color—so long as it is ultra-soft and machine washable (babies will be babies, and babies spit up). For the sample, I used the following:

- Lion Brand Homespun (98% acrylic/2% polyester; 185 yds/170g per skein): 1 skein Cobalt #379
- Bernat Soft Bouclé (100% acrylic; 225 yds/140g per skein): 1 skein Beautiful Blue #26116
- Lion Brand Microspun (100% microfiber acrylic; 168 yds/70g per skein): 2 skeins each Lilac #144 and Buttercup #158; 1 skein Mango #186

You might want to compare yarns as a group before you get started. A good way to see all the colors together is to take a snippet from each ball and paste it to the diagram. This is also a good way to make sure you have each block assigned—some people might take on more than one.

Needles

Whatever size needles work best with your chosen yarn(s) as determined by swatching; different weights of yarn will require different needle sizes.

Notions

Tapestry needle, crochet hook for edging (optional)

Gauge

It might seem silly to knit a gauge swatch for something that's little more than a swatch itself, but in this case it's important, both to determine the needle size necessary to get a fabric that you like as well as to determine the number of stitches per inch in your pattern. Remember to knit at least a 4" square with at least one full repeat of your pattern—a swatch of stockinette stitch will tell you nothing about the gauge for *your* pattern stitch.

Pattern Notes

- To break up the standard grid of afghan squares, I've developed a pattern of blocks laid out in a herringbone pattern (see diagrams). Most of the blocks have a width-to-length ratio of 2:3; for the sample, I worked blocks with a 2:3 ratio that measured 6" x 9". A few are longer and some are square, just to fill in the edges. You can cast on for the long or short edge, whatever works for your pattern. The size is big enough to really get the feel for a new pattern but small enough to complete in an evening or two.

- The small blanket measures 24" x 30"—perfect for tucking around a brand-new person in a stroller or car seat. To make a larger blanket, either increase the size of the blocks, maintaining the ratios (e.g., 8" x 12"), or use the larger pattern, which uses more blocks.

Instructions

Small Blanket: Work 13 blocks as follows: 8 rectangles with a ratio of 2:3 [6" x 9"]; 3 rectangles with a ratio of 2:4 [6" x 12"]; and 2 rectangles with a ratio of 2:2 [6" x 6"].

Large Blanket: Work 22 blocks as follows: 15 rectangles with a ratio of 2:3; 4 rectangles with a ratio of 2:4, and 4 rectangles with a ratio of 2:2.

Determine Your Cast-On Stitch Count

After working your gauge swatch in the yarn and pattern stitch that you'll be using, decide whether you want to cast on the long or short edge of your block. Then determine the number of stitches needed for that edge. You'll usually want to maintain full multiples of your repeat (it's pretty hard to break up a cable in the middle). Also, take into account that you'll need a border on all sides of your knitting. The border should be a plain stitch, such as stockinette, garter, or seed stitch. This acts as an anchor to your pattern and provides a selvedge, or seam allowance, for sewing the pieces together.

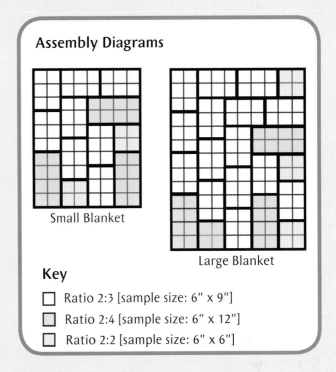

Assembly Diagrams

Small Blanket

Large Blanket

Key

☐ Ratio 2:3 [sample size: 6" x 9"]
☐ Ratio 2:4 [sample size: 6" x 12"]
☐ Ratio 2:2 [sample size: 6" x 6"]

Example: 18 stitches of your chosen stitch pattern in the yarn of your choice = 4". You plan to cast on 6", so based on your gauge, that will be 27 stitches. Your pattern has a repeat of 6 stitches.

Now you need to fudge a little bit. 4 repeats of your 6-st pattern will give you 24 stitches, so you'll need to decide whether you want to have a 1- or 2-stitch stockinette stitch border on either side of the pattern stitch, for a total of either 26 or 28 stitches. There's no exact formula for how many plain stitches to do on the sides—this is knitting after all, not rocket science. In this case, I'd go for the 2-stitch border and 28 total stitches because you will "lose" 2 of those border stitches when you sew the pieces together. That's your cast-on number.

Now, cast on the number of stitches determined in the exercise above.

Work your chosen border stitch for 2–4 rows.

Work your pattern, remembering to include the border stitches on either side, until you are nearing the required length for your block.

Finish up the row repeat, if any.

Work your border stitch until the block is the correct length.

Bind off.

Finishing

Block all pieces to the appropriate measurements.

Draw straws or otherwise determine who will sew everything up. Lay out the pieces as shown in the Assembly Diagram. Sew the pieces together firmly, but don't pull the yarn too tightly when seaming because you want the edges of the pieces to remain elastic.

Work a border of your choice all around the blanket. I worked a few garter-stitch stripes in different colors and mixed it up a bit by putting eyelets [yo, k2tog] in one of the garter stripes. Remember to increase 1 stitch at each side of the corners every other row so that they will lie flat. For a finishing touch, I worked 1 round of single crochet, then 1 round of reverse single crochet. This is a nice, though completely optional, touch—after all, for many of us knitters, crocheting is a "new skill" that we can add to our repertoires!

Knit a Blanket for Charity

Do you feel inspired to knit a baby blanket? Consider donating it to one of the following organizations, which accept hand-knit blankets. Be sure to check with the charitable organization before you begin knitting. Many have guidelines for hand-knit donations.

Project Linus
www.projectlinus.org
Project Linus' mission is to provide love, a sense of security, warmth, and comfort to children who are seriously ill, traumatized, or otherwise in need through the gifts of new, handmade blankets and afghans. Visit the site for free blanket patterns and links to local chapters.

Newborns In Need
www.newbornsinneed.org
Newborns in Need is a 501(c)3 charity organized to take care of sick and needy babies and their families; and in cases of crisis, to help where help is needed. Learn how to help at their website.

Free Baby Blanket Patterns
www.knittingpatterncentral.com/directory/baby_blankets.php
This page features links to dozens of free baby blanket patterns.

A Note to My Friend Who Knits

by Rachel Cottone

For your beautiful gift, I thank you.

I can easily picture you knitting this blanket for me, cuddled in a big chair in your house with the boys running trucks over your feet. Or maybe this is a gift started long ago, when you still lived in New York City and would knit standing up in a subway car. (How did you ever keep your balance?) Whenever and wherever you made it, I'm grateful this gift made its way to me at last.

You knit this lovely thing in entrelac, braiding the yarns together into a basket pattern. As I touch it, I can't believe anything so soft and precious is mine. I don't want to put it down. Can I just keep holding it?

When I think about precious gifts, I remember your baby shower. Remember that day? It was good to come together with your friends, sisters, aunts, and mom to talk, laugh, and eat cake in the shape of a stork, while you opened gift after gift.

In the midst of the celebration, an older woman who knew me better than I knew her leaned over and whispered in my ear, "I heard about your miscarriage. This must be hard for you."

Afterward, she leaned back, peered at me a little, and did what you don't hear many women do at a baby shower. She quietly told me the story of her own loss, twenty years earlier. And it happened again later in the kitchen with your sister. She poured a cup of coffee, sipped it slowly, and told me her story. By the end of the baby shower, five women in the group had taken me aside to acknowledge my experience and share theirs. In the midst of the joy for the new baby, we made room to honor the babies we lost.

Strangely, our moments of sadness together made us all the more grateful and joyful for the baby that was coming to you. It was not hard to find a smile to meet yours.

I have to finish writing now because I hear my own baby crying. In a moment, I'll wrap her in your blanket and tell her how lucky we are to have friends who keep us warm.

Elizabeth Zimmermann/ Meg Swansen Knitting Camp

by Mary Langevin

Before the Internet, there were no blogs, correspondence was via the postal service, and most knitters that I knew enjoyed their craft in the solitude of their homes. Okay, maybe we might run into each other at the yarn store, but to meet for coffee and take out your knitting . . . not exactly. My initial experience in a knitting community started at Knitting Camp, and I have never looked back.

I first heard about Knitting Camp in the early 1980s. As I had only two to three weeks of vacation, it didn't fit my schedule or youthful instinct for adventure. Then I saw it mentioned in the *Knitter's* Winter 1998 issue, and my interest was piqued. Elizabeth Zimmermann's camp was still going after all these years and was now being run by her daughter, Meg Swansen, and her company, Schoolhouse Press.

Knitting Camp is a mix of camp structure, knitterly nonconformity, and magic. Thursday is an evening to renew old friendships, make new acquaintances, begin to admire others' knitting, and feast on Schoolhouse Press eye candy—yarn, books, and special items. A whole room is set up with their products, including Elizabeth Zimmermann and Meg Swansen *original* knitted items. This is not for the faint of heart. Seeing these masterpieces (after loving use and many washes), along with the vast array of colorways, tugs not only at one's creative soul, but also at one's checkbook. If campers are worried about buying too much yarn at once, Eleanor, Michelle, and Tami, who manage much of Schoolhouse Press' business aspects, have been known to organize "Secret Shetland Shipments." These are necessary for knitting campers who exceed the unwritten, unspoken camp budget. More important, shipping logistics must be tightly coordinated to occur when one's husband is away on business, in order to reduce those looks that imply one's stash may be out of control. (Don't ask how I know about these things.) Amy and Joyce, both expert knitters and teachers, are available to any knitter for one-on-one assistance. It is a very open, friendly environment, where knitters approach each other, ideas are exchanged, and fiber and technique are everyone's passion. In fact, every night, after groups of knitters have "invaded" Marshfield restaurants en masse, they return to the Great Knitting Room.

Typically, classes start at 9:00 a.m.; it is camp, after all. Meg, with the video camera aimed at her hands and four large TV monitors placed strategically around

the room, demonstrates a host of techniques. Meg is a technical genius. To experience her charm, creativity, and encouragement, attendance is *de rigueur*. Since this is a group of knitters, it is *very* interactive. Around 10:30 a.m., there is a coffee/tea/cookie/fruit break, where tables are set up to encourage conversation. (Everyone wears a self-designed nametag, which helps congeniality.) Sometimes, the class photo is organized during this session; other times, Eleanor is chasing campers for the "Brown Book." Every camper has a page, where Schoolhouse Press orders are recorded, items taken from the Schoolhouse Press tables are logged in (everything is on the honor system), and questions or topics for Meg are registered. This is to ensure that she covers everything of interest and that orders are packed in a timely manner. Class then continues until noon or so.

After lunch, there's a short break, followed by show-and-tell. This is an opportunity for campers to troubleshoot problems, show works-in-progress, and modestly brag about some successes. I have seen some incredible trunk shows. When you live in the Midwest and drive to camp, you are limited to the vehicle's capacity. I leave it to the reader's imagination.

Usually on Saturday afternoon, there is a vendor market, where local suppliers set up their wares. My favorites include Jan Kimmet (Bohuslike yarn), Mielke's Farm (unbelievable homemade soaps—I stock up for a couple of years), and Joslyn's Fiber Farm. Needless to say, stash accumulation management is severely challenged.

The literature promoted the Knitting Camp experience as "in the middle of nowhere," which I interpreted to mean that I'd have an uninterrupted week of knitting. For someone living in New York City, that sounded pretty relaxing and stress-free. Fuhgeddabout it! Since there have been a number of non-knitting-related episodes over the years, it's hard to imagine a camp session involving only knitting. Usually, there's always something that helps to "label" the session. On my first trip out to Marshfield, Wisconsin, the connector flight was supposed to disembark us at the Mosinee (CWA) airport, in the middle of ginseng farms. Not tonight, we were told. We did an emergency landing in Appleton because this was

Camper, Linda Chism, shows her version of EZ's Pi Shawl at Camp, July 2007. *Photograph courtesy of Meg Swansen*

"Tornado Alley" in the summer. When I at last arrived, I learned that all the other knitters were assembled in the one hotel corridor that had no windows. They had brought their needles, good humor, and a knitting bagpiper.

There was the year of the hazmat (hazardous materials) cleanup at the hotel where camp was run at the time. As I understand it, a little too much chlorine was put into the pool, and in minutes, the bunny-suited professionals arrived. Luckily, all guests were evacuated and no one was injured. On short notice, the owner of an office building next to the hotel permitted the vendor market to relocate, and when every possible sale was closed, knitters sat in the parking lot, admiring their purchases and each other's beautiful creations. Knitting Campers not only made the front page of the local newspaper that year, but also the evening news. One year Knitting Camp was held in October, and we were treated to fourteen inches of snow! Then there was the year when we closed the Great Knitting Room around 11:00 p.m. and moved over to the bar for a few nightcaps. I managed to leave my purse on the floor and take my knitting bag and card key to my room . . . always keeping those priorities straight. The next day, the desk clerk called me over and asked me if had forgotten something. I showed her my knitting bag, she showed me my purse, and we had a good laugh.

Every year, I meet incredible people who share this passion and yet have other lives outside of knitting. (Imagine?) Highly talented women and men from all walks of life, all parts of the United States, and even other countries come to Marshfield for this experience. I remember one woman who talked like a truck driver and knitted like an angel—her lace shawls and tablecloths were the most exquisite pieces that I have ever seen. Ever. Another was a stay-at-home mom who seemed unsure about her life choices, along with her knitting. During her show-and-tell, she pulled out the most detailed Norwegian sweaters, one after another. The oohs and aahs from the crowd seemed to be a confidence-building experience, and not only for her beautiful knitting.

Blogs, chat rooms, and e-mail sustain me when I'm between camp sessions. But for me, sitting in front of the computer isn't the same as sitting in the Great Knitting Room, with my feet up and my needles clicking happily on my current

"Every year, I meet incredible people who share this passion and yet have other lives outside of knitting. (Imagine?) Highly talented women and men from all walks of life, all parts of the United States, and even other countries come to Marshfield for this experience."

Each year, Retreats 2 and 3 have a contest. The topic is selected at the end of each session, so Campers have a year to knit their entries. The topic of Masks was selected for the camp contest in July 2005. *Photograph courtesy of Meg Swansen*

project. I know that there are fancier places than Marshfield, but I look forward to the Friday fish fry at 13th Street, Monday send-off breakfast at the Kitchen Table (Meg's sister's restaurant), and Culver's, the custard place. These rituals keep Knitting Camp comfortable. Yet, campers, old and new, keep learning, experimenting, and sharing, which keeps Knitting Camp fresh and interesting.

And did I mention that Sue, the local massage therapist, sets up her chair at the back of the room so you don't miss any part of the class? Better get in line.

For More about Knitting Camp

Schoolhouse Press
www.schoolhousepress.com
The Schoolhouse Press website contains information about all their publications, as well as the camp.

Sweaters from Camp: 38 Color-Patterned Designs from Meg Swansen's Knitting Campers
by Amy Detjen, Meg Swansen, and Joyce Williams, published by Schoolhouse Press, 2002

Chapter Three
Needles, Yarn, and Politics

Think politics has no place in a knitting circle? Think again. Using knitting to make a political statement is nothing new—remember the colonial women who rebelled against the Stamp Tax by choosing to spin their own yarn and knit their own clothing rather than buy English goods. This chapter explores the ways in which knitting circles continue to raise awareness and change the world with yarn and needles.

Revolutionary Knitting

by Yin Ho

The spirit of revolutionary knitting is found in the roots of peaceful activism and opposition, from Betsy Ross sewing up the first American flag to the Granny Peace Brigades silently knitting in folding chairs near the White House to protest the Iraq War. Textile protest is not new: The early nineteenth-century Arts and Crafts movement arose in response to the immense changes of the Industrial Revolution. The objective at that time was to showcase beautiful creations of craftspeople that factory production could not hope to emulate. The contemporary movement expands upon that spirit to encourage a "constructive revolution" where knitters produce their own goods with political intention. The G8 summit in Calgary in 2002 first drew the Canadian Revolutionary Knitting Circle into the public eye. Since then, craft as activism around the globe has pushed the privacy of knitting into the forum of public protest. Revolutionary knitters use their craft as a medium of social change.

When knitters collectively share a political intention, they organize in a number of ways. Chapters of the Revolutionary Knitting Circle organize "sit-ins" in protest of corporate slavery and for peace and activism. The demonstration is a knitting performance, inviting spectators to observe and even take part in a more human form of production. In New York, Cat Mazza invited knit and crochet hobbyists to contribute small squares to a petition for fair labor policies at Nike. The signed squares were assembled into a blanket petition showing the Nike corporate logo. Mazza traces such forms of social protest back to French philosopher Felix Guattari's idea that "social change happens through small acts of resistance." Slight shifts in perspective can lead complacent consumers to become political producers.

What is it about knitting that makes it a perfect revolutionary vehicle?

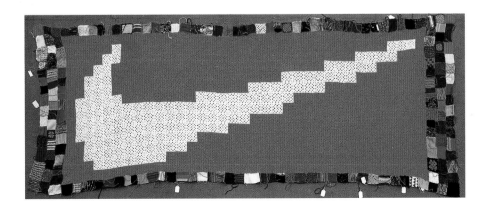

For More about the Revolution

Follow the revolutionary activities of Cat Mazza and Lisa Anne Auerbach.

MicroRevolt
www.microrevolt.org
See the Nike Petition, browse a calendar of revolutionary knitting events, and read Cat Mazza's blog.

Lisa Anne Auerbach
www.lisaanneauerbach.com
See Lisa's projects and read the "Little Red Blog of Revolutionary Knitting."

Opposite page: Lisa Anne Auerbach created *My Jewish Grandma is Voting for Obama, Is Yours?* in response to a video by Sara Silverman encouraging young Jewish Americans to convince their grandparents to vote for Barack Obama. The sweater and skirt set was machine knit in wool in 2008. *Photograph by Lisa Anne Auerbach*

Left: Cat Mazza's blanket petitions for fair labor practices at Nike. *Photograph by Cat Mazza*

1. It is self-reliant. Knitting means creating something, and creating it yourself. In this era, the Revolutionary Knitting Circle's manifesto states, that's akin to a revolutionary act. Knitters are familiar with the effort involved in making, and they can see an item from start to finish. Revolutionary Knitting Circle protests often display this simple resourcefulness by quietly knitting as a group to demonstrate their alarm at pervasive consumerism. Dependence on purchasing so much of what we need from distances farther and farther away disconnects us from the process of making, and from our own self-reliance.

2. It imparts value. Sweatshop labor lowers the cost of many goods, making buying more attractive than making. For instance, my mother thinks, "Why knit booties when I can buy them? Time is money!" Mother used to think of booties as a sweet gift made with care for friends' and relatives' babies, and she knew firsthand the time and craftsmanship put into a pair. Now, she sees how much hand-knit baby booties go for today, and it affects her decision to knit or to buy. The revolutionary knitter, however, still picks up those needles; doing so outweighs passive low prices with active ability. As a result, the revolutionary knitter recalibrates the booties' value.

3. It is farsighted. Apparel purchases are made with thrift and trends in mind, and then easily forgotten once the season has run its course. With such a fleeting purpose, it's not surprising that the care with which merchandise is made has declined. Revolutionary knitters assert that it is far more rewarding to maintain objects of craftsmanship for years or even decades. As a protest to the growing shoddiness of contemporary society, making durable items means longer usage and minimized waste.

4. It encourages community. Knitting circles offer a community of like-minded individuals the chance to meet and act as a group, encouraging more than knitting—the groups share a mindset that cherishes action and a do-it-yourself nature. This pooling of resources enables communal self-sufficiency and presents a practical alternative to the multinational corporate culture that these circles wish to dissolve.

5. It can be a platform. Lisa Anne Auerbach spreads the revolutionary spirit by example. The L.A.-based photographer and knitting artist knits sweaters, hats, mittens, and more, emblazoned with political statements. She knits in public, "not as a statement, per se, though I understand how it can be read as such," and in private. She encourages knitters to take up arms with their needles, "chart your message, and wear it proudly." The degree of personalization and effort involved in knitting gives a sense of urgency and importance to these messages that differs from a message screen-printed onto a T-shirt.

If we are mindful that any chosen medium can carry a message, the road to revolution is well-paved.

Oppposite page: Freedom is Messy/Shoot to Kill sash is Lisa's commentary on the Iraq War. It was machine knit in wool in 2005 by Lisa Anne Auerbach. *Photograph by Lisa Anne Auerbach*

Recipe for Activist Knitting

1. Organize your call to action—what is it that you are broadcasting or protesting?
2. Impassion yourself and others to your cause.
3. Consider your avenue for dissent—how will you act (e.g., knit a sweater, plan a sit-in, create a collective project)?
4. Create, create, create!

Tic Tac Tote Bag

Design by Vyvyan Neel

This tote bag is perfect for getting a whole group involved in one project. Individual squares are worked up and sewn together patchwork style. Since it is felted, any small difference in gauge from knitter to knitter will disappear. Different color schemes can be tailored to the recipient, whether girl, boy, or adult. Since the squares make a grid, it creates an ideal game board for playing tic-tac-toe.

Number of Knitters
Three to thirty. Squares, handles, and playing pieces are all knitted independently.

Finished Measurements
18" wide x 6" deep x 24" high **before** felting
13" wide x 4½" deep x 15" high **after** felting

Materials
Yarn
7 colors of worsted weight yarn in an animal fiber; all colors should be the same type of yarn to ensure that the pieces felt at a similar rate. The yarns used in the sample are the following:
- Brown Sheep Lamb's Pride Worsted (85% wool/15% mohair; 190 yds/4 oz per skein): 2 skeins Deep Charcoal #M-06 (A); 1 skein each Royal Purple Flutter #M270 (B), Cranberry Swirl #M250 (C), Ocean Waves #M220 (D), Prairie Goldenrod #M240 (E), Blue Skyways #M230 (F), and Orange Creamsicle #M280 (G)
- DMC Cotton Perle 3 (100% cotton; 27.3 yds/5g per hank): 1 hank Red #321 (or strong thread in coordinating color)

Needles
Size 10 (6mm) needles

Notions
Size G/7 (4mm) crochet hook, blunt tapestry needle, sharp tapestry needle, zippered mesh laundry bags and/or pillowcases

Gauge (pre-felting)
16 sts and 32 rows = 4" in garter st.
Gauge is not critical for this project; make sure that your stitches are loose and airy.

Pattern Notes

- If a different yarn is substituted, it is recommended that all colors be the same brand to help ensure that the felting will be uniform.
- When working a striped square, do not break yarn when changing colors; carry it up along the outside edge.

Instructions

Solid Garter Squares

Make 21 Solid Garter Squares in the following colors: 6 B, 2 C, 4 D, 3 E, 3 F, 3 G

With designated color, CO 22 sts.

Work in garter stitch (knit every row) for 38 rows.

BO on RS row.

Striped Garter Squares

Make 8 Striped Garter Squares in the following colors: 1 A/C, 2 A/D, 2 A/E, 1 A/F, 2 A/G

With A, CO 22 sts.

Row 1 (WS): Knit.

Rows 2 and 3: Knit with designated contrasting color (C, D, E, F, or G).

Rows 4 and 5: Knit with A.

Rep [Rows 2–5] 7 more times.

Rep Rows 2–4 once more.

BO on WS row with A.

Striped Mitered Squares

Make 8 Striped Mitered Squares in the following colors: 1 A/B, 2 A/C, 1 A/D, 2 A/E, 2 A/F

Note: Change colors at the beginning of every RS row.

With MC, CO 41 sts.

Row 1 (WS): Knit.

Row 2 (RS): With designated contrasting color (B, C, D, E, or F), k19, S2KP, k19—39 sts.

Row 3 (and all WS rows): Knit with same color as on previous row.

Row 4: With A, k18, SK2P, k18—37 sts.

Row 6: With contrasting color, k17, S2KP, k17—35 sts.

Continue in this manner, alternating colors on each RS row and knitting 1 fewer st before and after the double decrease with each succeeding RS row until 3 sts rem and you are ready for next RS row.

Last row: Do not change to A; with contrasting color, SK2P, then break yarn and fasten off.

Handles, Make 2

With D, loosely CO 100 sts. Work in garter stitch for 12 rows. BO loosely on RS row.

X's, Make 6

With E, CO 16 sts.

Beginning with a WS row, work in St st for 3 rows. BO all sts. Piece measures approx 4½" and will curl up on itself to RS. Make another piece in the same manner. Weave in loose ends. Overlap these 2 pieces in the shape of an "X" and tack together in the center.

O's, Make 6

With E, CO 30 sts.

Beginning with a WS row, work in St st for 3 rows. BO all sts. Piece measures approx 8" and will curl up on itself to RS. Sew short ends together to form an "O."

Finishing

Assembly

Refer to diagram for placement of squares. Butt edges of 2 squares together and, using a blunt tapestry needle and A, whipstitch them together. When all squares are sewn together, whipstitch the side of the bag to make a tube, then whipstitch the tube to the remaining 3 edges of the bottom to complete bag shape. *Note: 2 solid B squares will remain—set aside and do not felt! These will be used later to make a small pouch for the tic-tac-toe pieces.*

Weave in any loose yarn tails. Do not attach handles until after felting process.

Felting

Place all pieces (bag, handles, X's and O's, but not 2 rem squares) into several zippered mesh bags or pillowcases. Fill a top-loading washing machine with hot water to a medium water level and add a small amount of detergent. Put the bags or pillowcases into the water and agitate. Check the felting process every 5–10 minutes and remove pieces when they are the desired size; reset agitation cycle as necessary to continue felting. Do not use the spin or rinse cycle because that could create creases in the fabric that might not come out later. Rinse the pieces in cold water, gently pressing or squeezing out excess water. You may need to tug the bag a little to set back to a rectangular shape. Stuff bag with loose filling, such as plastic grocery bags, so that it holds its shape while drying, but leave spaces for air circulation. Clothespins can be used to create creases at the sides and bottom, but remove them while the bag is still slightly moist or they may leave indentations.

When dry, fold top set of squares in half to the inside of the bag. Cut slit openings along fold line just big enough for straps to fit through (see diagram for handle placement). Unfold top of bag, slip handles through slits and using sharp tapestry needle and Cotton Perle, sew handles to inside of bag. Fold top of bag back down, matching up the squares at the whipstitch line. Using Cotton Perle, whipstitch edge down, sewing through only part of the bag thickness to prevent stitches from showing on the outside of bag.

Game Piece Pouch

Stack the 2 remaining solid B squares and whipstitch around 3 edges using desired color of yarn. With crochet hook and desired color of yarn, make a crochet chain 32" long. Break yarn and weave in ends. With blunt tapestry needle, weave the chain in and out of the fabric at the top edge of pouch to make a drawstring closure. Loop one end of chain around handle on bag and tie chain together at ends. Put game pieces inside pouch for storage.

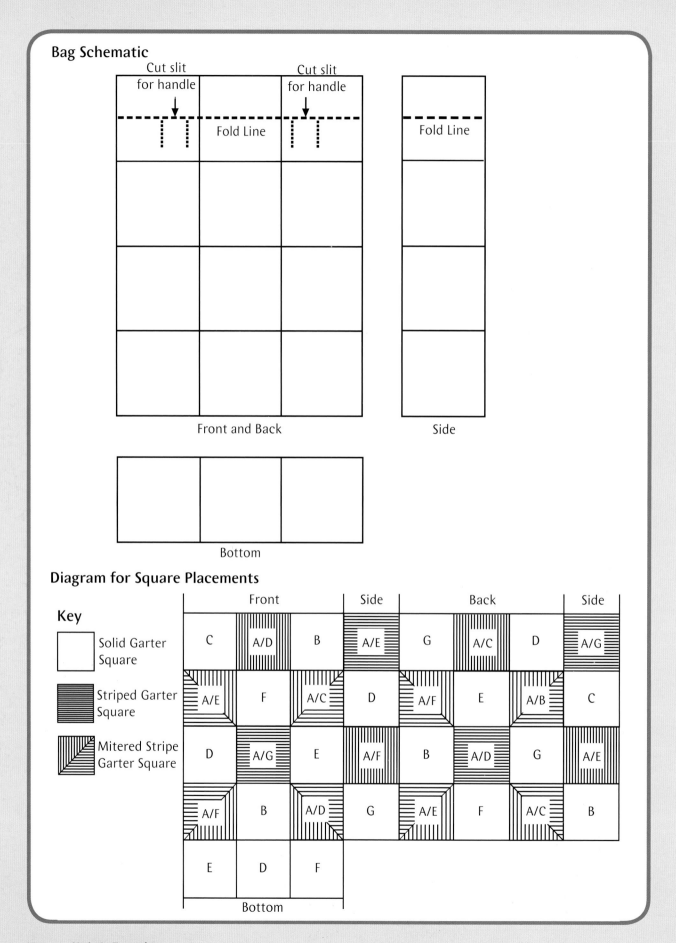

Bag Schematic

Cut slit for handle

Cut slit for handle

Fold Line

Fold Line

Front and Back

Side

Bottom

Diagram for Square Placements

	Front			Side	Back			Side
	C	A/D	B	A/E	G	A/C	D	A/G
	A/E	F	A/C	D	A/F	E	A/B	C
	D	A/G	E	A/F	B	A/D	G	A/E
	A/F	B	A/D	G	A/E	F	A/C	B
	E	D	F					

Bottom

Key

Solid Garter Square

Striped Garter Square

Mitered Stripe Garter Square

A Knitted River

by Graham Turnbull

On a Saturday in May 2007, I walked along a river in a park near Vauxhall station in south London. The river had not existed a year earlier. It was not the result of the floods that sometimes make the news here. It was made entirely of yarn. I was one of more than 250 people who had come to help carry this river over the Thames, past the Houses of Parliament, and up Whitehall to 10 Downing Street. It was a knitted petition, or *knitition*, as it came to be known.

The mile-and-a-half walk from Vauxhall to Downing Street was meant to be symbolic of the daily journeys made by millions of women around the world to collect water for their families. The time wasted is time that cannot be spent caring for their children. Children miss out on school. Crops are not tended. Walking miles every day to collect water is just one of the ways in which a billion people around the world are caught up in an endless cycle of poverty.

The river was made up entirely of squares of knitted fabric, some 100,000 of them. At the time, I estimated the river to be almost a mile long. It was sewn in blanket-sized sections to make it easier to carry through the busy streets of central London. London is used to people marching on its streets—we had a full police escort, marshals wearing yellow vests, organizers with megaphones, and even curious tourists looking on from open-topped double-decker buses.

Only a year earlier, Gerard Allt and Craig Carruthers, the owners of I Knit London, an innovative knitting café and sanctuary, had sent out this simple message to the two hundred or so members of their customer mailing list:

Around 100,000 squares were sewn together to create a river almost a mile long. *Photograph by Graham Turnbull*

We need as many knitted blue squares, 15cm x 15cm, as possible. Any shade, yarn or pattern, the squares will be sewn together to make a river. I hope the river will be big enough to make such a splash that we will walk it through London in a peaceful demonstration. The river will also be used for future WaterAid campaigning and events.

WaterAid is an International organization working in 17 countries in Sub-Saharan Africa and Asia. Over the past 25 years WaterAid has helped over 20 million people gain access to life saving clean water, hygiene and sanitation education. It is the world's foremost water and sanitation charity.

I will provide some blue yarn but if you could start making them and bring any along to this and future meetings I would love you even more. Squares can also be posted to me so please tell as many knitters as possible. We need to make a global impact.

Gerard knew all about WaterAid and its work. He had been a longtime volunteer with the water charity and had recently started working for them full time in their campaigns department. The original goal of the river campaign was to collect five thousand squares to represent the five thousand children who die from water-related poverty every day.

I first met Gerard and Craig working their stall in London's famous Spitalfields Market. I had only just started knitting myself, and I was surprised to see two other men involved in the pursuit. They invited me to join their mailing list, and soon I was invited to knit with them in busy, smoky, central London pubs. Those pub meetings became the source of the river. People would drop by after work to have a drink, socialize, and knit squares. This generated a few dozen squares, which Gerard and Craig would take home and sew together. I remember the first time I saw the river. It looked a bit like one of my own unfinished knitting projects. The campaign had just started, and it all fit into a black garbage bag. It would not be very long, though, before Gerard and Craig could no longer carry their knitting project around with them.

In England, when you are not home, your postman leaves you a red card telling you that a package has arrived for you, and you have to go to the post office to pick it up. Initially, Gerard and Craig were quite excited about going to the post office to pick up the parcels of squares that started coming in from all over the world. Eventually they got tired of it and, presumably, so did their postman, who had to fill out a red card every time a mailing arrived. Gerard and Craig decided to have the squares mailed directly to WaterAid, where volunteers could sort through them and continue sewing them together.

The first square from outside of the knitting circle came in from Texas. Nobody knows how someone in Texas found out about the campaign. Knitting friends started asking me about the campaign, knowing that I had appeared with Gerard

The river formed the center of a peaceful demonstration to bring awareness to water poverty around the world. *Photograph by Graham Turnbull*

in a video entitled *Men Who Knit* a few months earlier. I was surprised that the news of the campaign was spreading so quickly.

I suspect many of the squares came from the Women's Institute (WI), a powerful political organization with membership of more than 200,000 women, made famous in the United States thanks to the movie *Calendar Girls*. The Middlesex, Wisconsin, chapter alone contributed one thousand squares. One member who had fallen and broken her hip used her time in convalescence to knit squares for the river.

An entire school in Cumbria learned to knit so that they could contribute squares. A group of women, celebrating a friend's sixtieth birthday in a cottage in upstate New York, took yarn and needles and spent the weekend knitting squares. Squares also came in from as far away as Australia and New Zealand. A Men Who Knit club in San Francisco sent in squares as well.

What surprised me was the diversity in the squares. If I were asked to knit a blue square, I would have found a nice blue yarn in the bottom of my knitting basket, picked up some size 13 needles, and done alternate rows of knitting and purling until I had a six-inch (15 cm) square. I would have cast off and sent it on its way. It would not have occurred to me to knit a square with a fish on it, or to knit a square with different shades and kinds of yarn, or to knit a square in which you could see the waves in the pattern or hear the ocean by holding up a square with a seashell motif to your ear.

The river had its own blog. It had a MySpace page. It was written up in knitting magazines and blogs around the world. Squares continued to flow in to London even after the initial purpose of the river had been fulfilled. How do you stop a river? The WaterAid website announced that the campaign was closed, but the squares kept coming.

> **"I was especially touched and impressed by the children who learned how to knit in order to contribute to the project. In the run-up to the big march, Gerard and Craig still had thousands of unsewn squares, like so many unfinished knitting projects. They enlisted the help of local schoolchildren, who sewed them up by the bag."**

What made people go to the trouble of knitting a square and sending it all the way to London? Perhaps people had heard about the tank in Denmark covered in a pink blanket as part of an art project and peace protest. Perhaps lots of people really like to knit but do not necessarily want to take on a big project. With the Internet and twenty-four-hour television, it is impossible not to know what is going on in the world. People give money to charities, but many feel frustrated knowing that there are fundamental reasons for poverty that require the cooperation of entire nation states before they'll ever be resolved.

I was especially touched and impressed by the children who learned how to knit in order to contribute to the project. In the run-up to the big march, Gerard and Craig still had thousands of unsewn squares, like so many unfinished knitting projects. They enlisted the help of local schoolchildren, who sewed them up by the bag. The secondary school students wanted to know what the project was all about, so Gerard talked to the school about WaterAid's mission, raising awareness of schools in the same neighborhood as the WaterAid offices. Gerard and Craig were acting locally and thinking globally at the same time.

At the end of the march, a small contingent took a framed fragment of the river to Number 10, where it was accepted by one of Tony Blair's aides.

Since the march, the river has appeared all over the capital and farther afield. I once saw it draped over the fly tower of the National Theatre, appearing as if a waterfall were flowing down over the theater and collecting in a pool outside the espresso bar.

The river is currently being divided up into blankets to be distributed to homeless and animal welfare charities across the United Kingdom.

Craig and Gerard's tradition of knitting in pubs on Wednesday nights alternates now with knit-ins at their shop, I Knit London. Thankfully, the pubs are no longer smoky.

For More about Knit a River

Visit the following websites to learn more about the Knit a River project and the organizations involved.

I Knit London, a shop and sanctuary for knitters
106 Lower Marsh, Waterloo, SE1 7AB
www.iknit.org.uk
www.myspace.com/iknitlondon
Keep up with the happenings at Craig and Gerard's London shop.

Knit a River Blog
http://knitariver.blogspot.com
Although the project is over, you can still read all about it here.

WaterAid
www.wateraid.org/
Learn about WaterAid's mission, donate, and get involved.

Tree of Life Banner

Design by Suzyn Jackson

Inspired by the Knit a River and Nike Petition projects, I designed this knitted tree. It could be donated to a local school or eco-charity to be used as an Earth Day (April 22) awareness piece, or it could become a decoration for a child's room.

The tree can be as large or as small as you like. The leaves are quick and fun to knit, and they could be sent in from any number of knitters. The trunk is a larger piece and should be completed by a single knitter.

The tree scales easily. While the instructions will produce a tree about four feet tall, a single knitter could create a knitted bonsai fairly quickly.

Number of Knitters
Three or more. Each knitter knits one or more leaves. One knitter can knit the trunk and branch, or several people can knit additional branches.

Finished Measurements
Leaves: 1–4" depending on yarn and needles used
Trunk and Branches: As big or small as you like; sample is 32" tall

Materials
Yarn
Leaves: Any yarn you like, so long as it's green. This is a great way to use up odds and ends in your stash. You could also create an autumnal tree using a range of yellows, oranges, reds, and browns. Plan on 100–200 leaves for a 4-foot tree. Of course, a tree with more leaves will look more lush!
Trunk and Branches: Any yarn you like, so long as it's brown. Inexpensive acrylic works just fine. If different knitters use different yarns for the branches, all yarns should be approximately the same weight. In the sample pictured, I used a worsted weight yarn:
• Caron Perfect Match (100% acrylic; 355 yds/7oz per skein): 1 skein Espresso #7772

Needles
Leaves: Whatever needles work with your yarn
Trunk and Branches: Size 10 (6mm) 24" circular needle; if using a different yarn, use needles 1 or 2 sizes larger than called for on the yarn label; you want a loose fabric that will stretch.

Notions

Tapestry needle, at least 2 yards of heavy burlap, a broom handle or a dowel 4 feet long and 1″ in diameter; sewing machine (optional)

Gauge

Leaves: Not critical—whatever works for your chosen yarn.

Trunk and Branches: In the sample pictured, 16 sts and 20 rows = 4″ (10cm). If using a non-worsted-weight yarn, you'll need to determine your own gauge so you can figure out how many stitches to cast on, decrease, and increase; you should be aiming for a loose fabric.

Special Abbreviation

S2KP2: Sl 2 sts together knitwise, k1, pass the slipped stitches over; this makes a centered double-decrease. The raised center stitches form a vein along the length of the leaf.

Pattern Note

The pattern instructions for the trunk and branches are based on a gauge of 4 sts = 1″. If your gauge is different, or if you want a larger or smaller trunk, you'll need to adjust the number of stitches. The trunk is a concave shape, with a bottom width of 24″, decreasing to 8″ about 2/3 of the way up, then increasing to 16″ at the top. It should not be perfectly symmetrical, but you can do your own thing—after all, every tree is unique.

Instructions

Leaf

Make as many as you can; the sample has more than 100.

Leaving a 4–6″ tail, CO 3 sts.

Row 1 (WS): P3.

Row 2 (RS): Sl 1, yo, k1, yo, k1—5 sts.

Row 3 and all WS rows except where indicated: Sl 1, purl to end.

Row 4: Sl 1, k1, yo, k1, yo, k2—7 sts.

Row 6: Sl 1, k2, yo, k1, yo, k3—9 sts.

Row 8: Sl 1, k3, sl 1, k4. (On Rows 8 and 9, you're slipping the center stitch.)

Row 9 (WS): Sl 1, p3, sl 1, p4.

Row 10: Sl 1, k2, S2KP2, k3—7 sts.

Row 12: Sl 1, k1, S2KP2, k2—5 sts.

Row 14: Sl 1, S2KP2, k1—3 sts.

Row 16: S2KP2—1 st.

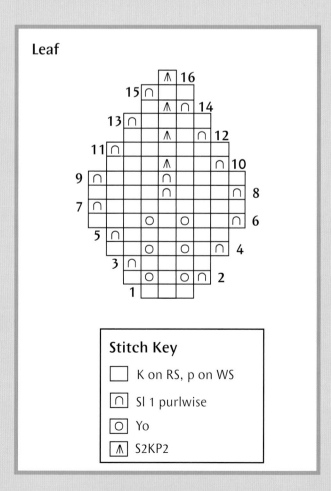

Leaf

Stitch Key

☐	K on RS, p on WS
⋒	Sl 1 purlwise
○	Yo
⋀	S2KP2

Cut yarn, leaving a 4–6" tail for attaching the leaf to the burlap. Fasten off last st.

Trunk

CO 96 sts.
Working in St st, decrease on both sides, quickly at first and then more gradually. Aim to have approximately 32 sts by the time the trunk is about 18" long. For the next few inches, continue to decrease slowly on one side and increase on the other side at the same slow rate (this will make the trunk tilt slightly to one side). Finally, increase on both sides, slowly at first, then increasingly quickly until the piece is approximately 32" long and has 64 sts across the top. Bind off.

Branch

CO 15 sts.
Working in St st, make a centered double decrease (S2KP2) in the middle of every other RS row until 1 st remains. Fasten off last st.

Finishing

Put small weights on the bottom corners of the trunk and hang by the top corners for about a week. This will stretch the knitting out of shape.

Arrange the trunk, branch, and leaves on the burlap; the sample has the purl side of the trunk and the knit side of the branch facing up—it's knitter's choice. Using a tapestry needle and brown yarn, sew the trunk and branch to the burlap. Tack through the middle of the trunk as well, so that it does not sag off the burlap when hung. Using a tapestry needle, draw the top and bottom tails on each leaf through the burlap. Carefully turn the burlap over and lightly knot the leaf tails together, taking care not to cinch the burlap.

Hem the bottom and sides of the burlap. Fold back the top 4" of the burlap and sew to WS, forming a tube. Slide the dowel through the tube and hang by the dowel.

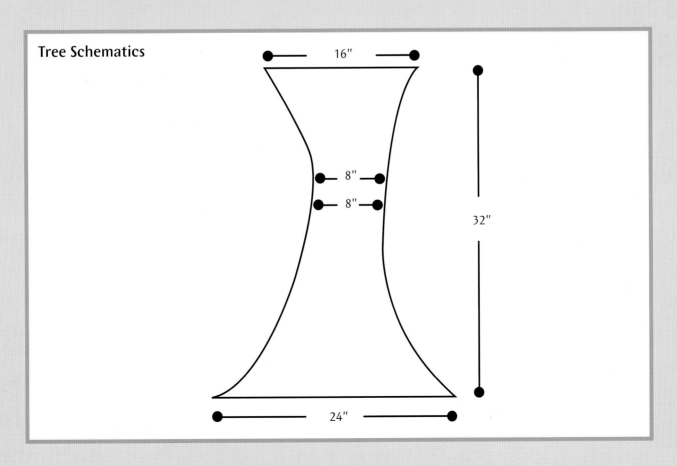

Tree Schematics

16"

8"

8"

32"

24"

Fighting Poverty with Art

by Suzyn Jackson

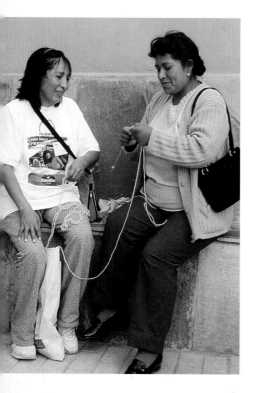

Long a traditional craft, knitting is now a viable source of income for the women of Ayacucho, Peru. *Photograph by Michael Smith*

Lydia was born high in the Andes, the rugged and mountainous countryside of Peru. She lives in the town of Ayacucho with her husband and three young children. Like many Peruvian women, she learned to knit from her mother and grandmother.

Life is difficult in Ayacucho. It was the birthplace of the Shining Path, the communist guerilla group that formed in the early 1980s. Between the group's terrorist activities and the government's violent response, the Peruvian countryside was ravaged. Approximately 70,000 people died or disappeared during the 1980s and 1990s. Ayacucho is the second-poorest province in the country; more than half of its residents live below the poverty line.

The disparity between rich and poor is felt keenly in Peru. Because of limited budgets, public schools only provide a half-day of school. Private schools are expensive, but they are the only option for a quality education that could lead to a professional job. In fact, keeping their children in school is most families' primary strategy for escaping poverty. But even an education is no guarantee of a better life. Formal sector jobs are scarce in Ayacucho, and the capital, Lima, is oversaturated with graduates unable to find jobs. So many families rely on small businesses to scrape together a living.

Knitting is a traditional craft in Peru, but given the fierce competition and lack of demand in local markets, it is almost impossible for artisans to earn a living wage. Many artisans work seventy-two hours per week—that's twelve hours per day, six days a week—to earn a gross income of less than $200 per month. Subtract the cost of their materials, and they earn a profit of around $60 per month. In contrast, the legal minimum wage is about $150 per month for a forty- to forty-eight-hour work week.

About five years ago, Lydia joined a microfinance organization called FINCA Peru. FINCA Peru is a nonprofit bank that provides credit through an empowering education program to women struggling to support their families. Since it was founded in 1993, FINCA Peru has served more than 20,000 clients and has won prestigious awards from the Inter-American Development Bank, the Microfinance Information eXchange, and the United Nations. As a client of FINCA Peru, Lydia received small loans and attended weekly meetings, where she received training and support. Importantly, she and the other clients were required not only to pay back their loans but to save a portion of their incomes each week—a new concept for many clients.

Lydia used her loans to invest in her small business of making cheese to sell in the local market. She also knits, constantly—she literally walks down the street knitting. For many years, she attempted to sell her work by knocking on neighbors' doors, but they could not afford to pay her a livable wage.

The leaders of FINCA Peru recognized that many of their clients were skilled artisans who simply lacked a market for their work. In 2006, they formed FINCA Peru Exports, with a mission to "provide our artisans with the tools necessary to overcome their poverty. FINCA Peru Exports is committed to fighting poverty with art, by offering our artisans access to Fair Trade markets, training and support and a fair price for their work." When FINCA Peru's international volunteers announced a knitters' group, Lydia jumped on the opportunity.

Both FINCA Peru volunteers and the artisans had their work cut out for them. The women had no idea what products, designs, or materials would be appealing to the North American and European markets. They mostly knitted sweaters, hats, and scarves of cheap wool and synthetic yarns, relying on traditional patterns. An easy first step was to switch to alpaca yarn, which is native to Peru and can be as soft as cashmere. Volunteers researched designs that were selling well in fair trade stores. Without abandoning their traditional colors and patterns, the group was soon making winter hats, gloves, shawls, and scarves.

Another consideration was the skill level of the artisans. At weekly training sessions, more experienced knitters helped the others improve their techniques and learn new stitches. This training was an important step toward producing consistent products for export.

Finally, FINCA Peru Exports helped to create a business structure. They outlined reasonable expectations, helping the group to set deadlines. They helped the women to calculate their costs of production and provided contact with fair trade distributors, such as Lucuma Designs and One World Projects, which recognized FINCA Peru's track record. Because FINCA Peru had to balance a commitment to paying the artisans a fair wage with the need to sell products at a certain price point, the women learned to work with greater speed and dedication, to finish orders on time and to a high level of quality.

Lydia has used her savings to improve her family's house, adding a roof of corrugated metal. When her husband became ill, she was able to pay for his medical bills and support the family. She has even paid off the mortgage on her house. Her goal is to save $3,000 to put her children through college. It may sound like a modest goal, but she has been working toward it for years, and it will take her many more years to achieve it.

Today, the knitters' group meets every Saturday and often during the week to come up with new designs, to fill existing orders, and to receive training. Their meetings are a mix of work and social time. The women are most comfortable speaking in Quechua, the ancient language of the Andes, which dates back to the time of the Incas. The artisans realize that they are stronger when they work together. By collaborating and sharing resources and expertise, they all benefit.

Just as important, or perhaps more so, the women are learning to value themselves, their talents, and their work. Their traditional "women's work" is paving their way out of desperate poverty.

To Learn More

Would you like to learn more about microfinance and support knitters in the developing world? Here are some websites to start your education.

FINCA Peru Exports
www.fincaperuexports.org
Shop the latest catalog of crafts by artisans like Lydia.

One World Projects
www.oneworldprojects.com
Get more information on fair trade products.

Kiva
www.kiva.org
Fund your own microloan to an entrepreneur in the developing world.

In FINCA Peru's knitting group, more experienced knitters help others to hone their craft. *Photograph by Michael Smith*

Stripes and Spots Toy

Design by Suzyn Jackson

Newborn babies can't see very well. Not only do they need to learn to use the muscles that control their eye movements and focus, but they also have to build the connections in their brains that help them understand what they are seeing. Visual stimulation is crucial for this process, and high-contrast patterns provide the strongest stimulation.

This is the idea behind this little toy. That, and the fact that I love a gender-neutral baby gift that isn't green or yellow!

Baby gifts make wonderful group projects; they're small, so they're quick to knit, but they're also incredibly meaningful to both parents and babies. This toy has a different stimulating black-and-white pattern on each side. The sides are knit separately, then joined to form a cube.

Number of Knitters
One to six. Each knitter knits one or more sides of the toy.

Finished Measurements
Approx 3½" cube (if using Lion Brand Microspun)

Materials
Yarn
Any soft machine-washable sport weight yarn will work. You'll need 1 ball each of black, white, and red, and you'll have plenty left over. The yarn used in the sample is
- Lion Brand Microspun (100% microfiber acrylic; 168 yds/70g per skein): 1 skein each Lily White #100 (A), Ebony #153 (B), and Cherry Red #113 (C)

Needles
Use needles one or two sizes smaller than called for on the yarn label; you want a nice, firm fabric.

Notions
Tapestry needle, stuffing (such as Poly-fil™), a sheet of upholstery foam (optional), a jingle bell (optional), crafter's glue

Gauge
28 sts and 36 rows = 4" (10cm) in stranded St st.
It's worth doing a gauge swatch and adjusting your needle size so that everyone working on the project achieves approximately the same gauge.

Pattern Notes

- The charts are worked using the Fair Isle or "stranded" method of knitting with multiple colors; this requires that you carry both colors (black and white) across each row.
- The red border on either side of each square is worked using the intarsia method of knitting with multiple colors. Use separate balls of yarn for the border and do not carry the yarn across the back; instead, bring the new color being used up and around the yarn just worked; this will "lock" the colors and prevent holes from occurring at the join. Before you start knitting, make a second small ball of red.
- You can knit this toy with any weight of yarn, but if you do, alter the measurements given below as necessary.

Instructions

Make 6 squares, 1 from each of the charts.

With C, CO 27 sts.

Knit 1 row, purl 1 row.

Next row (RS): K3 C; work Row 1 of one of the charts over the next 21 sts (for the 6-st repeats, you'll repeat the pattern 3½ times); join the 2nd ball of C and k3 C.

Maintaining the 3-st St st border on each side, continue working the chart until the length of the interior pattern measures approx 3" or the same as its width, if using a different weight yarn.

With C, work 2 rows of St st.

BO.

Finishing

Block the pieces so they are all the same size.

Lay out the pieces as outlined in the diagram. This ensures that similar patterns are on opposite sides of the cube. Sew the pieces together into a cube, leaving 3 contiguous edges open to form a "lid." Refer to the Seams on page 134.

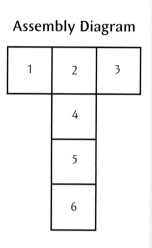

Assembly Diagram

1	2	3
	4	
	5	
	6	

For a square toy: Cut pieces of foam measuring approx 3½" square or whatever size will fit snugly into the toy. Cut enough pieces so that they will form a cube when stacked. Stick them together with a bit of nontoxic crafter's glue, tucking the jingle bell in the middle.

Lay a bit of stuffing in the bottom of the sack, then insert the foam cube. Tuck more stuffing down the sides to make it snug. Lay a bit of stuffing on the top of the cube, pull the lid down over it, and sew closed.

For a rounder ball: Simply fill the sack with stuffing, tuck in the jingle bell, then sew up the remaining sides.

Variation

Instead of a ball, make a book: Make 6–12 pieces (it should be an even number) and sew them all in a long strip with a few extra rows of red at one end. Fold the strip accordion-style. Sew the ends together—the extra red rows form the "spine" of the book. Sew the top and bottom edges of the "pages" together. Voila!

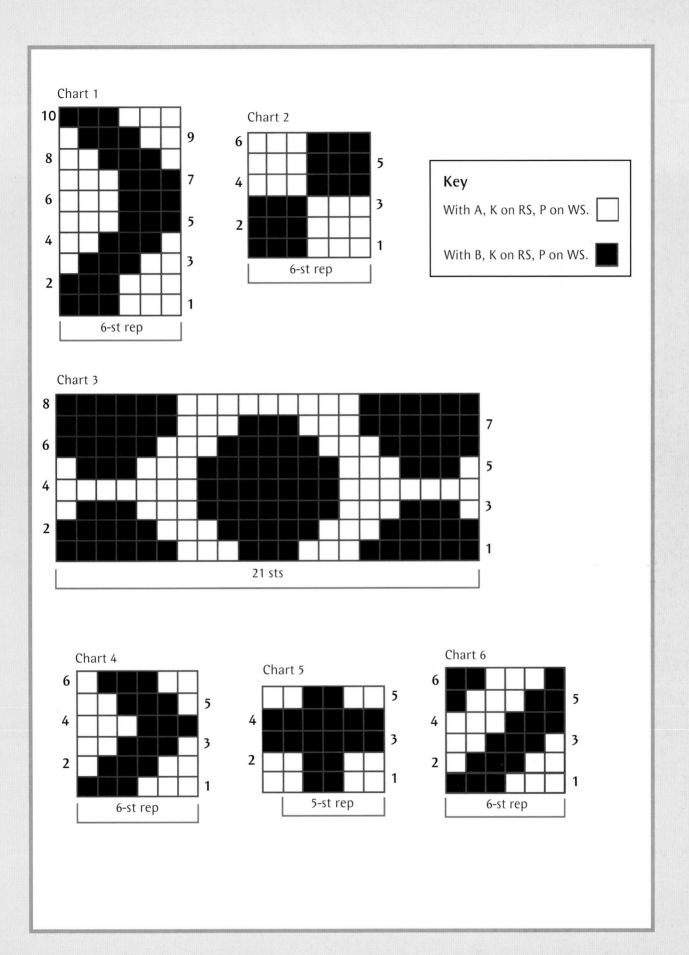

Chart 1

Chart 2

Key

With A, K on RS, P on WS. □

With B, K on RS, P on WS. ■

6-st rep

Chart 3

21 sts

Chart 4

6-st rep

Chart 5

5-st rep

Chart 6

6-st rep

Chapter Four
Knit Your Heart Out

Alvaro J. Gonzalez

Knitting for charity has been a theme of many knitting circles for well over a century, from bandages knit for soldiers during the Civil War to the afghans that are stitched together to warm those in need around the world today. This chapter explores the many ways that knitters give back to their communities.

The patterns in this chapter would make excellent gifts—to a charitable organization, to a local community effort, or to a friend.

From Social Knitting to Social Action: Organizing a Charity Knitting Project

by Tracy Sprowls Jenks

Many knitters feel the call to give away that which has been so lovingly knitted. It may be because they have extra balls of yarn left after finishing a project, or perhaps it's the urge to try out a new pattern. Maybe it is the desire to simply knit and, having done so many other projects, it makes sense to knit to give away. It could be—and I secretly think this has something to do with it—that knitters simply have big hearts.

There are many projects created by knitters to address needs and causes in the community. Babies need caps, people burned out of homes need blankets, and children all over the world need sweaters. For me, I was looking for a knitting project for two reasons. First, I wanted to genuinely make a difference in someone's life through knitting, which is my passion. Second, I was taking a self-expression and leadership program. The goal of the program was to demonstrate the power of the individual to make a difference in his or her local community and, in fact, the world. I needed to find a project as a practicum for the program.

After looking around on the Internet for a while, I came across the Caps to the Capital project that Save the Children sponsored in the fall and winter of 2006. This project was initiated after Save the Children released their report, "State of the World's Mothers," which noted that in developing countries, two million newborns die in the first twenty-four hours of life due to lack of warmth. Four million newborns die each year within the first month of life. Many of these babies could be saved if a few simple health measures were put into practice, such as providing antibiotics and immunizations, offering training to birth attendants, expanding education on breastfeeding, and giving lessons in basic care, such as keeping the baby dry and warm.

The goal of Caps to the Capital was to collect handmade knitted or crocheted caps from all over the United States and present them to President Bush with the idea of raising awareness of infant mortality and poverty. Afterward, the caps would be given to newborns in Bangladesh and Malawi. As of this writing, more than 280,000 caps have been lovingly knitted and sent overseas in hopes of preventing premature death in newborns.

I was excited by the Caps to the Capital idea—simply knitting caps drastically reduces infant mortality! So, I initiated a cap drive in my local New Jersey Unitarian Universalist (UU) congregations, called UUs Knit! My goal was to collect one thousand caps and send them to the Caps to the Capital campaign. Little did I know that knitters not only in New Jersey and New York but across the continent would be moved to knit baby caps. By the end of the drive, I collected 832 baby caps from local congregations as well as from states as far away as California. In fact, a friend in San Francisco called me during the cap drive to ask if I was going to participate in the UUs Knit! cap campaign. I laughed and told her it was my project.

So how do you start a knitting-for-charity project? Here are some simple guidelines:

1. Before starting a charity project, check to see if a program already exists. If so, then look for guidelines to starting your own branch of the program.

2. Determine a need or cause that lights you up and gets you excited. This could be anything! Baby caps for newborns, afghans for fire victims, socks for soldiers in combat, or chemo caps for cancer patients. Let your imagination run wild, but remember you must have passion for the project.

3. Decide if you wish to work with a group such as Save the Children or if you'd rather create your own group. If you work with another group, as I did, then you have a place to send your knitted projects. If you are not working with an established group, make sure there is a need for your item and a way to distribute it. This may involve several phone calls or e-mails. A contact person on the receiving end is very helpful.

4. Decide if you have specific requirements for the project, or check the organization's requirements on their website. If they do not have a website, be sure to contact them. Do afghan squares need to be a certain size? Do caps need to follow a particular pattern? Do socks have to be made out of a certain yarn? You need to be clear about instructions so that your knitters can send you what the project needs.

5. Set a goal. Do you want to collect one thousand caps? Knit a sweater for a child in need? Knit up six afghans? A clear goal helps motivate people and keeps you focused. The goal can always change. In some cases, you may fall short of your goal, as I did, but falling slightly short of a goal is better than having done nothing at all. Once the work is underway, anything can happen!

6. Decide how big you want your project to be. How many people do you want involved? Is this a project for your local knitting group or for a national organization? Will you have a deadline or is this an ongoing project? If you want your project to grow, determine needs such as a web page, chat lines, resources, mailing address, etc. For my project, I put the word out on a web chat I frequent. Because the project had a short time span, I did not set up a web page.

7. Develop a process to collect the knitted items. Be ready for a tremendous response! Where will the items be sent? Do you have a place to store items as they arrive? Will you sort through the items or will you have volunteers do it? For my project, I collected caps in my office and then mailed them to Save the Children. Sometimes organizations send thank-you notes from the recipients of

"By the end of the drive, I collected 832 baby caps from local congregations as well as from states as far away as California."

the knitted items. Collect stories and share them with those who knit for the cause.

8. Once you have finished your project (or once your open-ended project has been going for a while), assess the process. What went well? What could be done more efficiently or better? Are you still passionate and hungry for more? Does your project need to grow?

9. What is your next knitting-for-charity project going to be?

Although my project started in a congregation, knitting for others and special causes is not unique to religious communities. Any group can organize a knitting project in response to the needs of the world. I have heard of school groups, book clubs, women's groups, knitting circles, and yarn stores running various projects to fulfill a need. Women in nursing homes gather together to knit for newborn babies. The local craft store collects squares to sew together as afghans for shooting victims. The possibilities are endless. Any group can organize a charity drive. You simply need the idea, a goal, a way to share the message, and someone in need to receive the wonderful hand-knit treasures. Knitters are craving a way to give; all they need is to be asked.

Knitting for Charity

Opportunities for knitting for charity abound. Dive into this rewarding world. The following resources provide a number of ideas and tips for getting started. Or, simply type "knitting for charity" into any Internet search engine for more information than you could read in a lifetime.

Knitting for Charity: Easy, Fun, and Gratifying
www.knittingforcharity.org
A blog about charitable knitting, this site has links to charitable campaigns and free knitting patterns, as well as the author's musings on her own charitable knitting projects. For example, she lists tips for knitting blankets that will be appreciated by the many teenage boys that need warmth and assistance—but still want to be cool.

Daily Knitter
www.dailyknitter.com/charity.html
A list of charities from afghans for Afghans to Webb Babies, with a short description of each charity and a link to the charity's website.

Interweave Knits
www.interweaveknits.com/community/charities.asp
The publisher of a popular knitting magazine lists knitting charities on the web.

About.com: Knitting for Charity
http://knitting.about.com/od/knittingcharities/Knitting_Community_Knitting_for_Charity.htm
Another list of charities that accept knitted donations, this page also includes an excellent article:
http://knitting.about.com/od/knittingcharities/qt/charity_howto.htm.

Knitting for Others
www.knitty.com/issuefall03/FEATcharity.html
This article on Knitty.com lists more charities that accept knitted donations, as well as some thoughts on charitable knitting.

Knitting for Peace: Make the World a Better Place One Stitch at a Time by Betty Christiansen, published by Stewart, Tabori & Chang, 2006
A fabulous resource for the charitably minded, this book profiles charities that accept knitted donations and contains several patterns appropriate for giving.

Save the Children
www.savethechildren.org/campaigns/caps-to-the-capital
While the Caps to the Capital campaign is complete, Save the Children is running other campaigns that accept knitted baby caps. Visit the website for details, background information, patterns, and other ways to get involved.

You're the Love of My Life Baby Mobile

Design by Laura Brown

Baby mobiles are a fun addition to any baby's crib, providing entertainment and stimulation to the baby below. This sweet mobile features four hearts, which can easily be made by four separate knitters, each with a special connection to the new baby. What better way to express your love of knitting to the love of your life?

Number of Knitters

Two to five. Each heart is knit separately, and then there's all the I-cord.

Materials

Yarn

Four colors of whatever sport weight yarn you like. All knitters should use the same type of yarn. The yarn used in the sample is

- Debbie Bliss Baby Cashmerino (55% wool/33% microfiber/12% cashmere; 137 yards/50g per ball): 1 ball each purple #609 (A), lilac #608 (B), mint #003 (C), and pink #006 (D)

Needles

Size 3 (3.25mm) needles or size needed to obtain gauge

Notions

Size D/3 (3.25mm) crochet hook, tapestry needle, metal coat hanger or heavy-gauge wire, heavy-duty tape (e.g., shipping or duct tape), polyester fiberfill stuffing

Gauge

24 sts and 32 rows = 4" (10cm) in St st.

To save time, take time to check gauge.

Special Technique

4-St I-Cord: CO 4 sts. *K4, do not turn. Slip sts back to left-hand needle; rep from * until cord is desired length. Bind off or slip stitches to holder as indicated in pattern.

Pattern Note

In order for the mobile to function properly, each heart must weigh the same. Small differences in gauge between knitters can be offset by filling each heart with more or less stuffing, thereby making each heart equal in weight.

Instructions
Basic Heart

For all hearts, CO 1.

Starting with Row 1 (WS), follow chart.

On Row 27, work to center stitch and bind it off; join a new ball of yarn and continue working across the right side of heart. Working both sides at once, finish chart. *See below for colors for specific hearts.*

Embroidered Heart

Make 2 Basic Hearts, 1 with A, the other with B.

Use the photo as a guide for embroidery. With D, embroider two chain flowers on each side of heart. With C, embroider stems on each side using backstitch.

Textured Heart

Make 2 Textured Hearts, 1 with A, the other with D.

Heart with Dots

Make 2 Hearts with Dots, working the first side with A (MC) and B (CC) and the 2nd side with the colors reversed. Use intarsia method to work the colors (see Glossary).

Swirly Heart

Work first side with A (MC) and C (CC). Work 2nd side with A (MC) and D (CC). Use stranded method to work the colors (see Glossary).

Finishing (All Hearts)
Join Hearts

Place 2 corresponding hearts together with wrong sides facing out.

With crochet hook and B, work 1 rnd of single crochet through the slipped sts at the edges of both hearts until only 1" remains open.

Alternatively, using a tapestry needle, whipstitch the edges together.

Turn the heart right side out and fill with stuffing. Close the last inch.

Join another set of hearts with B, then join remaining 2 hearts with C.
Use crochet hook to draw all yarn ends inside hearts.

I-Cord Hangers

With D, work a 4-st I-cord 24" long. Bind off.

With B, work two 4-st I-cords 14" long; slip sts to a piece of waste yarn for holder.

With C, work two 4-st I-cords 12" long; slip sts to waste yarn.

Slip the 4 I-cords from waste yarn to needle, alternating colors B-C-B-C.

With C, k2tog across; do not turn—8 sts.

Slip sts back to left-hand needle and k2tog across again—4 sts.

Work 4 rows of 4-st I-cord.

Next row: K2, place rem 2 sts on safety pin.

Work 2-st I-cord for 6 rows. Break yarn and place these sts on another safety pin.

Slip sts from first safety pin to needle and work 2-st I-cord for 6 rows.

Slip the 2 sts from 2nd pin back onto the needle—4 sts.

Work 4-st I-cord on these 4 sts for 2 rows, then BO; this will form a loop for hanging the mobile. Weave in all ends.

Assembly

Straighten your coat hanger and cut a piece that measures 25" (1" longer than the longest I-cord). Thread the coat hanger into the longest I-cord, then shape the coat hanger into a circle and overlap the ends by 1". Tape the ends of the coat hanger together firmly. Pull the I-cord so that it completely covers the hanger. Sew the stitches from the beginning and end of the I-cord together. Weave in all ends.

Lay your 4 joined I-cords over the I-cord circle. Secure each I-cord onto the circle by wrapping in an X with A (use photo as a guide). Be sure to have an equal distance between the top of the mobile and the point where you secure each I-cord onto the circle. The B I-cords will hang slightly lower than the C I-cords. Weave in all ends. Attach each I-cord end to a heart edged in the same color.

Weave in all ends.

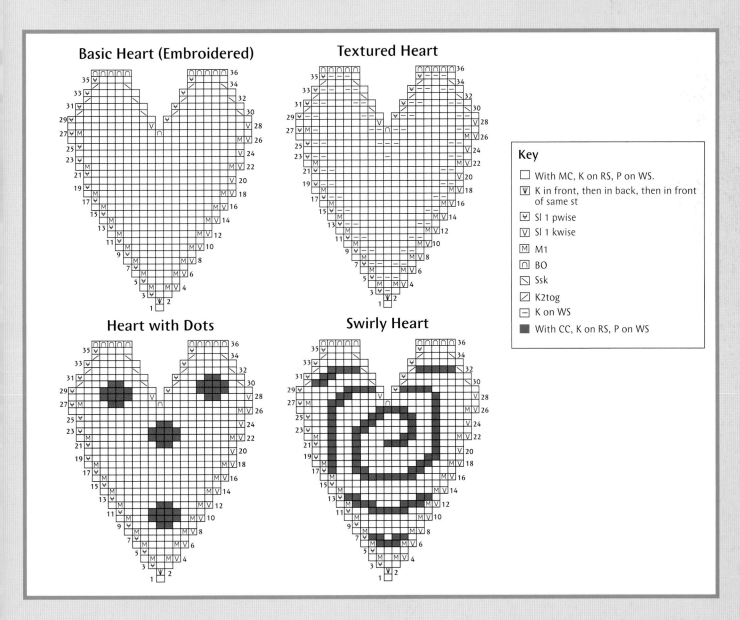

Basic Heart (Embroidered)

Textured Heart

Heart with Dots

Swirly Heart

Key

☐ With MC, K on RS, P on WS.

Ⓥ K in front, then in back, then in front of same st

☒ Sl 1 pwise

Ⓥ Sl 1 kwise

Ⓜ M1

⌒ BO

◺ Ssk

◿ K2tog

⊟ K on WS

■ With CC, K on RS, P on WS

The Power of Sheila's Shawls

by Greta Cunningham

This shawl, called *Harriet Tubman's Legacy*, was knit by Brian Jones, who works at the Harriet Tubman Shelter in Minneapolis. Reatha King purchased the shawl at the Sheila Shawl Extravaganza in 2004. *Photograph from the Silent Witness National Initiative for the Sheila Shawl Extravaganza, 2004*

On October 25, 2002, Sen. Paul Wellstone, his wife Sheila, his daughter, and five others died in a plane crash in northeastern Minnesota. Paul and Sheila were known for their work protecting women from violence. Friends of the couple say it was Sheila's urging that prompted Paul Wellstone to become a key Senate leader in crafting the Violence Against Women Act. Since their sudden death, friends of the Wellstones have been working to make sure their legacy stays alive.

Janet Hagberg lives on the eleventh floor of a high-rise building overlooking the Mississippi River and the skyline of downtown Minneapolis. She's the executive director of the Silent Witness National Initiative, a group that works to end domestic violence. Janet worked with the Wellstones on the issue. As she was coping with her grief over the Wellstone's plane crash, an idea for remembering Sheila's work occurred to her.

"I was wearing this shawl that I have in my hands; it's a wonderful soft, mohair shawl. And I was comforting myself in the loss of Sheila and just feeling sad and grieving. And it felt to me like Sheila was in the room with me when I was wearing this shawl, like I was really being comforted by her. And I thought, 'Oh, if I feel this much comfort wearing my shawl, how would it feel if you had lost someone to domestic violence?'" Janet says.

Janet's idea was to bring comfort—in the form of shawls—to people who have lost a family member to domestic violence. She calls them "Sheila's Shawls." She posted the idea on the Internet and enlisted the help of her knitting friends.

"I wear it even when I don't have to," says Irene Schneider, who was searching for comfort after losing her daughter, Megan Fischer, in a brutal murder. Irene's cousin, Betty, requested the shawl and asked that it be knit in Megan's favorite colors. When Irene is overwhelmed with grief at night, she grabs her dog, Giggles, and puts on her Sheila's Shawl.

"I see it and I go, 'Ah, Meg.' And I put it on and I walk around the house. I think of her a lot. I think of her all the time, and it's just like it's a moment between Megan and I," Irene says.

Megan was a lively, beautiful young woman who worked at a nursing home to support herself as she was going through chef's training at the Art Institutes International Minnesota. She graduated with honors from the culinary program and then landed her "dream job" as a chef at a nursing home. The job combined Megan's two passions: cooking and caring for the elderly.

"She was in seventh heaven," her mother says. "She got that job shortly after graduating and only had it for five months until she was murdered."

Megan Fisher was killed by a man she met in culinary school. He had spent time in the Schneider family home and had been invited to Megan's last birthday party. Irene says the man became enraged when Megan refused to let their friendship develop into a romantic relationship.

Phone records show that on the night Megan was murdered, the man was harassing her and calling her every five minutes. Megan had been refusing his calls, but cell phone records show she finally spoke to the man around one in the morning. That was the last phone call Megan Fischer answered. Megan's roommate found her lying in a pool of blood around 4:00 a.m.

"She had been stabbed seventeen times in her neck, back—and the most bizarre thing is the culinary kit that she had from school. He had gotten up and had gone into the kitchen and got that knife, and that's what he killed her with: her own knife. And that's how she died," Irene says. The man was convicted of first-degree premeditated murder. He is serving life in prison without the possibility of parole.

Megan's murder and the trial are part of a long string of misfortunes Irene Schneider has faced. Eleven years ago, her husband, Jim, Megan's father, died suddenly of a massive heart attack. He was a St. Louis Park police officer and died on the job at age forty-three. Five years ago, Irene was diagnosed with breast cancer. Through both tragic events, Megan was her pillar of support.

"And she would send me the funniest cards—from her heart—she would pour her heart out about how much she loved me and knew I was going to be okay because I was strong and I was a survivor, and now she's gone, and it's just so sad. It's just such a waste of a wonderful life. With Jim dying, with the cancer, and with Megan, it's like, okay, I'm done. I can't, I just don't want any more right now. Anyway, so I think of everything that she's ever done for me, said to me, given to me, hugged me, kissed me; it's all in the shawl. And that's what really makes it so special," she says.

Janet Hagberg, the organizer of the Sheila's Shawls program, says the volunteer knitters are asked to think healing thoughts and to try to knit love into each stitch. As a result, there's a powerful emotional connection between the knitter and the shawl recipient.

Connie Clarke has been knitting for charitable groups for the past forty years. She found out about the Sheila's Shawls program on the Internet and has donated twenty shawls so far. Connie said her motivation for participating was simple.

"I do it because it's something I feel can maybe make a difference in someone's life. I physically can't—I'm not out and around with people—but yet I feel I can create something that has a lasting comfort," Connie says.

Irene Schneider, still wrestling with her grief over losing her daughter, Megan, recognized that some people may not understand the comfort the shawls bring.

"I don't know. To me it's like I'm holding Megan when I hold that shawl. When I have it wrapped around me. And I just thank these lovely women that do this. And for the people that don't get it. Maybe it's a good thing because they haven't had an awful act of violence done to any of their loved ones. And I pray that they never do because it's unexplainable. It's a long haul and it's very draining. But the shawls help," she says.

How to Get Involved

Silent Witness Blog
http://silentwitness.wordpress.com
The Sheila's Shawls program is still active and accepting donations. Visit this site to learn how to get involved.

Sheila's Shawls Yahoo Group
http://groups.yahoo.com/group/SheilasShawls/?yguid=136299647
Receive updates and information on the Sheila's Shawls initiative by joining this Yahoo group.

Triangle Shawl

Design by Suzyn Jackson

A shawl is a gift of comfort, whether it is for a friend, or, through an organization such as Sheila's Shawls, for a complete stranger. Since this shawl can be knitted by a group of up to nine people, think of it as a group hug.

The pattern uses a simple lace pattern. Knit in a heavy yarn, it looks like retro macramé, though it's a lot softer than your grandmother's plant holder! Knit in a finer yarn, this shawl takes on the intricacies of a delicate spiderweb.

Choose colors that convey your wishes for the recipient—soft blues for calm, purples for introspection, greens for health, or a rainbow for vitality. Just about every tradition, from Wicca to feng shui, assigns meanings to colors. Go with your instincts—or simply ask the recipient what she'd like!

Number of Knitters
One to nine. Each knitter knits one or more triangles.

Finished Measurements
Sample measures approx 64" across top and 38" deep

Materials
Yarn
Any yarn you like. I've included a layout idea for three different colors, but you could use any number of colors between one and nine. I'd recommend that all yarns be the same weight so that one triangle doesn't pull others out of shape. Additionally, I recommend a yarn that contains some animal fiber so that the pieces can be blocked to the same size. In the sample pictured, I used the following:

- Lion Brand Wool-Ease Thick & Quick (80% acrylic/20% wool; 106 yds/170g per skein): 2 skeins each Raspberry #112, Wheat #402, and Fig #146

Needles
Whatever needles necessary to get desired fabric weight and drape with your chosen yarn. If multiple knitters are knitting the different pieces, you will need to adjust needle sizes to make sure that everyone achieves the same gauge.

Notions
Tapestry needle, stitch marker

Gauge
Once you have swatched your yarn and decide on a fabric that you like, make sure that everyone's gauge matches.

Pattern Notes

- Before you begin, calculate how many stitches will equal 18″ based on the gauge of the fabric that you have swatched.
- The sample was sewn together with the purl face as the "public" side, so that side has been identified as the "Right Side" in the instructions; you may decide that you would prefer the knit face as the public side—it's knitter's choice!

Instructions

Make 9 triangles, 3 each of 3 colors or as desired.

Triangle

CO 3 sts. Mark the center st.
Row 1 and all RS rows: Purl.
Row 2 (WS): K1, yo, k1, yo, k1—5 sts.
Row 4: K2, yo, k1, yo, k2—7 sts.

Row 6: K1, *yo, k2tog; rep from * until you reach the center st, yo, k1 [center st], yo, *ssk, yo; rep from * to last st, k1—9 sts.
Row 8: K1, *yo, k2tog; rep from * until you reach the center 3 sts, k1, yo, k1 [center st], yo, k1, *ssk, yo; rep from * to last st, k1—11 sts.
Row 9: Purl.
Rep Rows 6–9 until your piece measures 18″ across the top, ending with a WS row.
BO purlwise on the RS.

Finishing

Block all pieces. Assemble as shown in diagram with either RS or WS facing (knitter's choice) so that the outermost rows of holes line up. Using one long piece of yarn, sew all the pieces together working through the holes, following the path shown in the diagram. Weave in all loose ends.

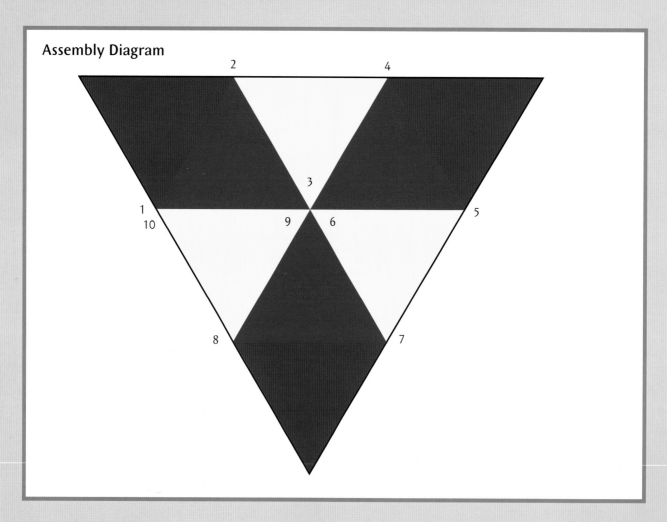

Assembly Diagram

Pretty Kitty Knitty Committee: Knitting for the Love of Cats

by Cindy Goldman and Cici Heron DeNovo

Overheard at a cozy coffeehouse in Portland, Oregon:

"Guess what? Malcolm and Daphne were having another one of their little spats yesterday."

"Uh-oh, what was it about this time?"

"It wasn't a big deal, just the usual: She thinks he's being a pest, following her around too much, so she feels she needs to put him in his place."

"So what did she do?"

"Well, she wrestled with him for a while and then she chewed on his ear a bit to teach him a lesson . . ."

No, this is not your typical coffee klatch; this is a Sunday afternoon meeting of the Pretty Kitty Knitty Committee (PKKC). The PKKC is a knitting/crochet group composed of volunteers from House of Dreams (HOD), Portland's only no-kill, free-roam cat shelter, which is home to Malcolm, Daphne, and dozens of other formerly homeless felines. The PKKC was started in 2006 by designer/author Kristin Spurkland, herself a HOD volunteer since 1999. At the monthly gatherings of the PKKC, up to a dozen members show up to practice their needlework skills while fashioning items that will be sold at the Pretty Kitty Holiday Craft Bazaar, House of Dreams' popular annual fund-raiser.

But making cat toys and hats and scarves for the bazaar isn't the only reason for the group's existence. "I wanted to give volunteers an opportunity to hang out and get to know each other, while also providing a casual forum to discuss shelter issues," says Kristin. "The primary motivation behind the PKKC is to foster community among HOD volunteers." Although the volunteers range in age (from eighteen to sixty-six) and come from a wide variety of backgrounds, the conversation is always friendly and upbeat, since all share a deep commitment to animals.

Daphne loves Kristin Spurkland's Double Knit Catnip Pillow (featured on page 93). Photograph by Alvaro J. Gonzalez

The knitters enjoy trading stories about both their own cats and the residents of the shelter while improving their knitting and crocheting skills. Cindy, a longtime volunteer, says: "We're really fortunate that Kristin's been so generous with her time and expertise; she's such a talented artist and a very patient instructor. I've always considered myself creatively challenged, so it's been a pleasure channeling my inner knitter with her help. And since many of us are only at the shelter one day a week, we might never get to meet one another if she hadn't organized the PKKC. Now we can pool our knowledge and resources, which benefits both the cats and the volunteers."

"The mission of HOD is to find loving, responsible homes for all the kitties it takes in, but because the shelter does not discriminate based on age or medical history, many of the cats are what some might call difficult to adopt. These special animals are welcome to spend the rest of their lives at HOD."

PKKC members' skill levels and experience also vary greatly. "My grandmother taught me to knit almost forty years ago, but I hadn't practiced since," says Debra, one of HOD's newer volunteers. "The PKKC has given me the opportunity to relearn the craft after all these years. Knitting with the group is another way to contribute to the shelter, and it allows me to socialize with other cat lovers." For Sharin, a college student who adopted a beautiful HOD calico named Pearl, knitting is a brand-new skill that didn't come easily. "It took me a long time to master the basic stitches," she says, "but I've been able to progress at my own pace without any pressure, and I've finally gotten the hang of it. I love coming to the meetings; besides knitting gifts to sell for the bazaar, I've even managed to make a cool scarf for myself."

An unexpected benefit of participating in the PKKC and volunteering at House of Dreams has been the way it has changed the volunteers' lives and attitudes. Sarah, HOD's volunteer coordinator, says, "I started volunteering because my love for cats is greater than my ability to take them in. The PKKC provides a wonderful outlet for my creative energies and a chance to talk about the shelter and all of the kitties we hold dear to our hearts." Shanna, the youngest knitter in the PKKC, began volunteering at the shelter as soon as she turned eighteen and soon adopted adorable Abby, a feline-leukemia-positive Siamese. "Volunteering at House of Dreams has changed my life entirely," she says. "I now fill up my free time with different shelter-related projects, such as writing for the newsletter and helping write grants. I never thought I'd be able to do so much, but this helps me make more productive use of my time. I've learned a variety of skills from these activities, and am still learning more each week."

All the efforts of the PKKC are geared toward improving the lives of the cats at House of Dreams. Operating with no paid staff, HOD is run by a team of dedicated volunteers. The shelter is a two-bedroom house furnished with lots of cat beds, handmade quilts, and scratching posts. The cats roam the house and find their own comfy hangouts, whether snuggled on a bed with several other cats or more quietly sheltered in a small box on top of the refrigerator; those who have tested positive for feline leukemia have their own cheerful room. The mission of HOD is to find loving, responsible homes for all the kitties it takes in, but because the shelter does not discriminate based on age or medical history, many of the cats are what some might call difficult to adopt. These special animals are welcome to spend the rest of their lives at HOD. At the shelter, they have friends (both human and feline), regular meals, a clean environment, and quality medical care. Also important for the cats' emotional well-being are the many volunteers who pet, groom, and talk with the cats, providing gentle attention and respecting each animal's individual personality and nature.

One recent success story is Liam, a sweet and loving older Manx with a big purr, who came to HOD after being rescued from life on the streets. Rough around the edges, with a cloudy eye, missing teeth, and the need to be on a special diet for the rest of his life, Liam was not an obvious candidate for adoption. But after he was featured in a story in the local paper, he was adopted by a wonderful couple who own a vegan restaurant in downtown Portland. They adore their new companion and claim that Liam is a music lover who especially enjoys Beethoven and Scottish tunes.

Yet even with happy endings like Liam's, volunteering at an animal shelter can be emotionally and physically draining, which is where a casual knitting group comes in. "It is my hope that the PKKC can add an element of relaxation, fun, and mutual support to the volunteers' work at House of Dreams," says Kristin. "It's been shown that people will stay with an organization longer if they form social bonds with their fellow volunteers. The PKKC is my way of helping to develop those important personal connections."

Learn More about House of Dreams

House of Dreams
www.kittydreams.org
www.myspace.com/
houseofdreamsshelter
P.O. Box 30971
Portland, OR 97294
503-262-0763

Pretty Kitty Knitty
Committee MySpace page
www.myspace.com/pkkc
Keep up with the doings of the Pretty Kitty Knitty Committee online.

Double Knit Catnip Pillows

Design by Kristin Spurkland for the Pretty Kitty Knitty Committee

Using the "double knitting" technique, these simple catnip pillows are easy and fun to make. Double knitting looks like flat knitting and is just as easy, but when you remove the knitting needles from the work, the knitting magically opens into a little knitted bag! Fill with batting and some catnip (or potpourri if the pillow is for people), add a French knot, graft the pillow closed, and you're done.

The pattern requires very little yarn, making it a great stash project. Once you understand the basic construction, you can easily adjust the size, shape, and colorwork to suit your needs.

These pillows are a perfect group project. The knitting is simple enough for those new to the craft, while more experienced needleworkers can do the grafting and add the French knots. Even nonknitting friends can help out by making the catnip/batting bundles for stuffing the pillows. Working in such an "assembly line" fashion, a group can make several pillows in one afternoon's knitting.

A collection of pillows makes a great gift for the new kitty owner or, if stuffed with fragrant potpourri, a lovely gift for a bride-to-be.

Number of Knitters
One or more. Each pillow is made by one knitter, but a group can quickly knit up a basketful.

Finished Measurements
Sample is 2" square. Can be made any size.

Materials
Yarn
Small amounts of stash yarn. Yarn can be any weight and fiber type—I prefer worsted to heavy worsted in natural fibers.

Needles
Set of needles 1 to 2 sizes smaller than the size recommended for your selected yarn; 1 spare needle the same size as project needles or 1 size smaller—this needle will be used as a stitch holder only

Notions
Tapestry needle; batting, fiber fill, roving, cotton balls, or whatever you want to use to stuff the pillow; catnip or potpourri

Gauge
Work at a firm gauge (not loose and open). That's why the pillows are knit in needles 1 to 2 sizes smaller than those recommended on the yarn label. Work a gauge swatch in St st to determine appropriate needle size and stitch gauge.

Special Technique
Double Knitting (even number of stitches)
All rows: *K1, sl 1; rep from * to end.

Pattern Notes

- You will be making a fabric that has the purl face showing on both sides.
- Double knitting requires working 2 rows (back and forth) to make 1 row of stitches, because you are only working half the stitches on each row and slipping the other half. The finished pillow will be half the width of your original cast-on width.

Instructions

Based on your gauge, CO 4" worth of sts, making sure it's an even number.

Work in double knitting until piece measures 2". Break yarn, leaving a 12" tail.

Divide sts onto 2 needles as follows: slip the first st onto one needle (needle A), the 2nd stitch on a 2nd needle (needle B), the 3rd stitch onto needle A, the 4th stitch onto needle B, etc., until all the stitches have been divided onto needles A and B (this is where your 3rd needle comes into use). If you've done everything correctly, your knitting should now open up into a little knitted bag.

Weave in ends, working them into the purl side of the fabric currently facing you. Keep your working yarn attached.

Keeping the stitches on needles A and B, turn the bag inside out so that the knit side is now facing out.

Stuff the lower half of the pillow as follows: Take some batting and fluff it out so it is in a flat "sheet." Put about a teaspoon of catnip in the center of the sheet, then fold the batting up around the catnip so it is enclosed. You now have a little bundle of catnip rolled up in batting, about half the size of your bag. Place this bundle in the lower half of the pillow.

Add lavender to the pillows to make sachets.

Make a French knot in the center of the pillow, working through both layers of knitting as follows: Thread yarn through a tapestry needle and bring the needle up through both layers of the pillow from the underside to the topside. Holding the yarn taut with your left hand, wrap the yarn around the needle twice (wrap more times if you prefer a larger knot). Maintaining the tension on the yarn, reinsert the tapestry needle through the pillow near the place where it originally emerged. Pull the yarn and needle through to the underside, making sure to hold yarn taut throughout. Tie yarn ends into a firm knot on the underside of the pillow. Make sure to knot the underside of your French knot securely, especially if your pillow is going to be a cat toy. Weaving in the ends alone will not be enough to keep kitty from pulling the French knot out of the work. Leave yarn ends about 1/2" long to ensure that the knot doesn't come undone.

Make a second catnip bundle to stuff the top half of the pillow. Add bits of batting as needed to fill out the pillow so it is adequately stuffed.

Close top of pillow by grafting or using 3-needle bind-off. Weave in tail.

To really scent the pillows, put them in a bag with catnip for a couple of days. Kitty will love it!

Options

You can make the French knot first, and then stuff the pillow. I find it easier to stuff, French knot, then finish stuffing, but you don't have to do it that way. Stuffing the pillow all the way and then adding the French knot doesn't work because it's very difficult to get the needle through the batting and catnip.

Catnip or Potpourri Bags

An alternative to making the batting/catnip bundles explained above is creating catnip bags out of old stockings. The bags don't fill the pillows as evenly, but they allow more of the catnip scent to permeate the pillow. You can use this technique for stuffing any kind of catnip toy or sachet.

Take an old pair of tights or stockings and cut off the feet. Cut the legs into short tubes 3" to 4" long. Place about a tablespoon of catnip or potpourri in the middle of the tube, then tie both ends off with an overhand knot. Place the bag into the pillow, then fill the rest of the pillow with batting as needed.

Imagine Muskoka

By Michele Meadows

K nitting and a love of nature are my true passions. These were the lures that brought me to Muskoka, Ontario, fourteen years ago. Shortly thereafter, I opened a knitting store, Muskoka Yarn Connection. Since then, I have been fortunate enough to combine knitwear design, teaching, and creative inspiration, while surrounded by the beauty of northern Ontario's majestic pines.

I started Imagine Muskoka, a community quilt project, in the spring of 2005. My idea was to inspire local knitters to create squares depicting favorite images of Muskoka, stretching their imaginations and working together to produce a one-of-a-kind work of art for charity. My customers constantly ask what to do with leftover yarns, and this was the perfect solution. Using a mixture of wool, cotton, mohair, alpaca, and acrylic in worsted weight, with textures ranging from eyelash to bouclé, I encouraged knitters to try intarsia and Fair Isle techniques with the occasional splash of embroidery for detail. I handed out flyers with a general

The finished quilt, depicting scenes of Muskoka life from canoeing to moose, was auctioned off to benefit the local hospital. *Photograph by Michele Meadows*

afghans for Afghans

www.afghansforafghans.org
afghans for Afghans is a humanitarian and educational people-to-people project that sends hand-knit and crocheted blankets and sweaters, vests, hats, mittens, and socks to the beleaguered people of Afghanistan.

outline of the project, stipulating eight-inch squares and a three-month deadline. There was no limit to how many squares each knitter could submit. With each completed square, knitters received a discount coupon for future yarn purchases.

More than one hundred squares were handed in, representing all aspects of Muskoka: a field of wildflowers, windswept pine trees silhouetted against an evening sunset, a red canoe, a lone fisherman, baskets of blueberries, cranberries representing our local marsh, dragonflies, moose, black bears, snowflakes, autumn leaves, birch trees in a winter forest, a bird's nest filled with tiny robin's eggs, and a log cabin nestled in the woods. Some knitters with less experience submitted solid color squares in a textured yarn or pattern, giving the illusion of waves on the water, an evening sky, and tilled soil on farmer's fields.

After the three-month deadline, I had the grand task of assembling the quilt. A panel of fellow knitters aided me in the choice and placement of each square. We picked squares that best represented the natural beauty of Muskoka and had a complementary color palette. It was a difficult undertaking to choose only forty-eight from the imaginative pile of more than one hundred squares. The quilt consisted of six squares across and eight rows down to make the finished size of approximately forty-eight by sixty-four inches. To stabilize the outer edges, I added a heavy stocking stitch border in denim blue worsted wool. I folded and sewed the top edge as a pocket for a wooden dowel, from which the quilt hung. To the back of the quilt, I added a piece of thick flannel, hand sewn along the outer edges. When we stood back and viewed the completed quilt, we were all genuinely impressed with the creativity and enthusiasm this project had generated.

Over the next few months, the quilt was on display in the front of the store as part of an exhibit entitled Knitworks. Friends and family members of the participants were drawn in to view the work. As word spread, tourists and cottagers soon started to appear, visibly enchanted by the tiny nature scenes and vivid details in each square. Our local newspaper featured the quilt in an editorial piece with color photos. Soon I had to start a list of names for advance ticket sales. The reaction was extremely pleasing, as what started as a charity project grew into a work of art, encouraging a cooperative spirit and true appreciation for the natural beauty of our area. After Christmas, I presented the quilt to the hospital auxiliary to be raffled off at their next luncheon. All money raised went toward much-needed new equipment for our local hospital.

Star Quilt Pillow

Design by Suzyn Jackson

This project is a knitted homage to that classic group activity, quilting. The individual pieces are knit to size, using different stitches to provide subtle interest. For a bolder effect, vary the colors for each piece.

The pillow would make an excellent housewarming or wedding gift, or it could provide a taste of home to a college student going off to the dorms. For a more ambitious project, a group could create several of these squares to make an afghan or blanket. Afghans make excellent charity projects, whether they are donated or auctioned.

Number of Knitters
One to eighteen. Each shape is knitted separately.

Finished Measurements
14" x 14"

Materials
Yarn
Smooth worsted weight yarns show off the different stitches nicely. In the sample I used the following:
- Patons Classic Wool (100% merino wool; 223 yds/100g per ball): 2 balls Aran #00202

Needles
Size 8 (5mm) or size needed to achieve gauge

Notions
Tapestry needles, 6 [1"] buttons, 14" pillow form

Gauge
14 sts and 18 rows = 3" in St st.

14 sts and 24 rows = 3" in seed and double moss st. It is important that you achieve both stitch and row gauge because the decreases must form a 45-degree angle in order for the pieces to fit together.

Pattern Stitches
Seed Stitch
Row 1: *K1, p1; rep from * across.
Row 2: *Purl the knit sts and knit the purl sts as established.
Rep Row 2 for pat, working new sts into pattern.

Double Moss Stitch
Row 1 (RS): *K2, p2; rep from * across.
Row 2: Knit the knit sts and purl the purl sts as established.
Row 3: Purl the knit sts and knit the purl sts.
Row 4: Knit the knit sts and purl the purl sts as established.
Rep Rows 1–4 for pat, working new sts into pattern.

Pattern Notes

- The front of the pillow is made up of 4 different shapes (a right-leaning trapezoid, a left-leaning trapezoid, a triangle, and a square), which are knit separately then sewn together.
- The pillow back is 2 rectangles, 1 of which has buttonholes.

Instructions

Trapezoid 1 (make 4 each in seed stitch)

CO 20 sts.

Row 1 (WS): Purl.

Row 2 (RS): K2, M1, work seed st to last 3 sts, k2tog, k1.

Row 3: P2, work seed st as established to last 2 sts, p2.

Rep Rows 2 and 3 until Row 23, with the following exceptions:

Rows 9 and 17 (every 4th WS row): P1, p2tog, work seed st to last 2 sts, M1, p2.

Row 24: BO knitwise.

Trapezoid 2 (make 4 each in double moss stitch)

CO 20 sts.

Row 1 (WS): Purl.

Row 2: K2, ssk, work double moss st to last 2 sts, M1, k1.

Row 3: P2, work double moss st as established to last 2 sts, p2.

Rep Rows 2 and 3 until Row 23, with the following exceptions:

Rows 9 and 17 (every 4th WS row): P2, M1, work double moss st to last 3 sts, ssp, p2.

Row 24: BO knitwise.

Triangle (make 4 in St st)

CO 29 sts.

Row 1 (WS): Purl.

Rows 2 and 4 (RS): K1, ssk, knit to last 3 sts, k2tog, k1—2 sts dec'd.

Row 3: Purl.

Row 5: P1, p2tog, purl to last 3 sts, ssp, p1—2 sts dec'd.

Rep [Rows 2–5] 3 times more—5 sts.

Row 18: K1, SK2P, k1—3 sts.

Row 19: Sl 2 sts one at a time knitwise, insert left-hand needle through both sts from right to left, remove right-hand needle, then p3tog; pull yarn through remaining st.

Square (make 4 in St st)

CO 3 sts.

Row 1 (WS): Purl.

Row 2 (RS): K1f&b twice, k1—5 sts.

Row 3: Purl.

Row 4: K1, k1f&b twice, k2—2 sts inc'd.

Row 5: P1, p1f&b, purl to last 3 sts, p1f&b, p2—2 sts inc'd.

Row 6: K1, k1f&b, knit to last 3 sts, k1f&b, k2—2 sts inc'd.

Row 7: Purl.

Rep [Rows 4–7] 3 times—29 sts.

Continue from Row 2 of the Triangle instructions above.

Back Pieces (make 2, one with buttonholes)

CO 65 sts.

Work K1, P1 rib for 1".

Buttonhole row (worked on only 1 of the pieces):

Work 6 [yo, k2tog] buttonholes evenly spaced across piece.

Continue in established rib for 1" (2" rib total).

Work in St st until piece measures 8".

BO.

Assembly

Block all pieces so that edges are the same length.

Match up one seed st trapezoid and one double moss st trapezoid along cast-on edges. Sew together (refer to Seams on page 134). Repeat for remaining pairs.

Arrange the 4 pairs of trapezoids as shown in the diagram. Sew together along the decrease edges.

Fit in the triangles and squares as shown, then sew together.

Sew bound-off edges of back pieces to top and bottom of quilt square. Sew along the side edges, overlapping the rib sections with the buttonhole piece on top. Sew the buttons onto the other rib piece, matching buttons up with the buttonholes. Insert a pillow form and button up.

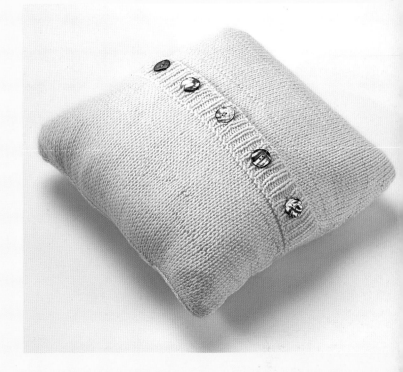

Assembly Diagram

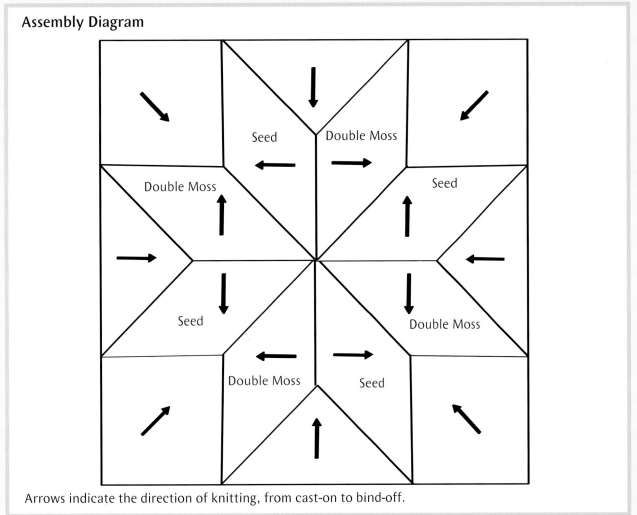

Seed

Double Moss

Double Moss

Seed

Seed

Double Moss

Double Moss

Seed

Arrows indicate the direction of knitting, from cast-on to bind-off.

Chapter Five
Around the Corner, Around the World

With the Internet connecting so many people around the globe, there's not much difference between around the corner and around the world anymore. This chapter explores the phenomenon of online knitting, where knitters from all ends of the Earth meet up and connect through blogs or at popular Internet sites like Ravelry. We also profile a project in London, which came together with the help of hand-knit contributions from around the world.

Unlike most of the group patterns in this book, the Global Baby Layette doesn't depend on joining pieces together, so it's a perfect project for a knitting circle that is spread around the globe.

Knit Your Own Ferrari

by Graham Turnbull

Twenty-two-year-old Lauren Porter wanted to do something different for her fine art sculpture degree course at Bath Spa University in Bath, England. She started exploring the idea of combining sculpture and knitting. She made a sink and a toilet, but Lauren thought that these domestic objects were still too close to the idea of knitting to make a powerful enough statement. Lauren wanted to get as far as possible from all that knitting was.

Nothing could be farther from the world of knitting than a high-performance car, and nothing says high performance quite like the Ferrari Testarossa. Lauren saw the Ferrari Testarossa as the most aspirational of consumer products.

Lauren decided that she would knit a Ferrari, an odd choice for a woman with no driver's license. She took the bus down to her local knitting shop and bought some red Sirdar acrylic yarn. When she went back for more, she found that the

Is it art? If it puts a smile on your face, Lauren considers it a success. *Photograph by Lauren Porter*

shop was all out. The story could have ended there, but Lauren called Sirdar. Not only did they have enough yarn (some twelve miles of the stuff), but when they heard about her project, they let her have it for free.

> **"Lauren needed to knit twelve miles of yarn into 250 squares (50 rows by 50 stitches of stockinette stitch on size 10 needles). She enrolled the help of her mother and three aunts. More people got involved, and, ultimately, people Lauren did not even know contributed squares. Some people learned to knit just so they could contribute a square."**

Making It

Just about anyone can learn to knit, and just about anyone who knits can knit a square of fabric. Thus, people working together can create large, beautiful pieces that would be too time-consuming to do on their own.

Lauren needed to knit twelve miles of yarn into 250 squares (50 rows by 50 stitches of stockinette stitch on size 10 needles). She enrolled the help of her mother and three aunts. More people got involved, and, ultimately, people Lauren did not even know contributed squares. Some people learned to knit just so they could contribute a square.

Lauren herself took on the trickier bits, including the window (and the windshield wipers!), the wing mirrors, and the famous horse emblem, which she embroidered by hand.

There is more to this Ferrari than brightly colored yarn. Lauren designed the frame herself. She looked up the scale measurements online, and she gleaned some of the trickier, curvy bits from a vintage 1980s Ferrari telephone. Then she enlisted willing fellow students to make it out of steel. After ten months, the result was a combination arts degree course sculpture, knitting circle collaboration, and dramatic statement.

What Happened to It?

Lauren's Ferrari went for a test drive at Bath Spa University's Fine Art Graduate Show in June 2006. From there, it accelerated up to the British International Motor Show, where it was displayed in a lineup of seven real Ferraris. Finally, in November 2006, it zoomed to the finish line when Lauren achieved her goal of getting her knitting into a fine art gallery in Mayfair, London's ultimate gallery district.

Unfortunately, it did not sell. The Ferrari is now being stored in a garage. Ferrari has been suspiciously quiet about the whole thing.

Lauren Porter and her friends knitted a Ferrari Testarossa out of twelve miles of Sirdar acrylic yarn. *Photograph by Lauren Porter*

But Is It Art?

When Lauren suggested to her tutors that she might knit her final project, they asked her, "Is knitting a craft or an art?" Lauren had always felt that "art should be for everybody." She thought that modern art is often quite depressing. She wanted to put a smile on people's faces. The owner of the gallery where the Ferrari went on show, Sarah Myerscough, said that the knitted Ferrari makes people question their perceptions about fine art. In convincing her tutors to let her show the Ferrari as her final project and in getting the Ferrari into one of London's top fine art galleries, Lauren has gone a long way in answering her tutors' question.

More about Knitting as Art

Lauren Porter's website
www.lauren-porter.co.uk
See more pictures of the Ferrari and Lauren's other knitted sculpture.

Knitting Art: 150 Innovative Works from 18 Contemporary Artists
by Karen Searle, published by Voyageur Press, 2008

KnitKnit: Profiles and Projects from Knitting's New Wave
by Sabrina Gschwandtner, published by Stewart, Tabori & Chang, 2007

Knit's a Small World After All

by Jacque Landry

"...Amy Singer bowled a strike when she first published Knitty in fall 2002. Her brainchild has given knitters all over the world a chance to come together and meet, learn, share, and form friendships with other people who understand the obsession that is fiber art."

Many knitters today did not gain their knit and purl know-how at the knee of a wise and experienced relative or friend. For a lot of people, it was Debbie Stoller and her phenomenally popular Stitch 'N Bitch series that enticed them to pick up the needles. Unfortunately, as good as those books are at preparing the rookie knitter for possible pitfalls, a book can only take a person so far.

Though knitting has really reemerged in popularity in the past several years, there are still many places without local yarn stores (LYS). Often, chain craft and bargain stores are the only sources for yarns, and their selection pales in comparison to what is typically stocked at an LYS. Many of these areas also seem to lack any sort of knitting community. Without a local knitting group or yarn store to turn to for help and reassurance, the next rational place to look for more information is the Internet.

Online knitting magazines such as Knitty.com, which has become the modern knitter's mecca, responded to the need for a reliable, twenty-four-hour knitting resource. If Ms. Stoller got the knitting ball rolling by tempting a whole new crowd of young would-be knitters to cast on, then Amy Singer bowled a strike when she first published Knitty in fall 2002. Her brainchild has given knitters all over the world a chance to come together and meet, learn, share, and form friendships with other people who understand the obsession that is fiber art. Knitters everywhere are grateful that Amy, who believes knitting is as essential as breathing, has brought such a valuable online magazine to the world of knitting.

Long before Knitty, there were knit bloggers. They were fewer in numbers than they are now but nonetheless committed. These were the fearless pioneers who braved the way for those of us who spend as much time in front of our computer writing and reading about knitting as we actually spend practicing our art. The concept of sharing personal knitting projects with complete strangers from all over the world is at once exciting and frightening. What if my projects aren't as well done as others out there, or, even worse, what if nobody cares? It is a scary thing to jump feet first into a blog, but when the first comment is posted saying, "That's a beautiful scarf," or "I love that yarn you used," the fear evaporates. Knitters are just nice people. About the only thing they like more than knitting is encouraging others to join in the fun. It may be a mad plan to populate the world with needle-wielding fiber artists, but I think there is just something comforting in the knowledge that there are others—many others—out there.

One of the most phenomenal aspects of the knit blogging community is the camaraderie and friendships that grow within it. People from all over the globe can find someone to identify with, and for many, it is these relationships that fill the void of local knitting support and resources. This tight-knit (pardon the pun) community is willing to share everything from advice and encouragement to tips on patterns, links to the best yarn sales, and even the occasional recipe. We swap e-mails, care packages, and sometimes yarn. More important, we are as interested in each others' lives as in each others' knitting.

Every day there are new developments enabling knitters and other fiber enthusiasts to connect via the World Wide Web. One recent online tool is called Ravelry, a free user-based knit and crochet community that has created quite a buzz among online knitters. The site was created by a knit blogger, her computer programmer husband, and their adorable dog, Bob, to fill the need for a knitting database. It gives knitters the tools to organize projects, stashes, needles and notions, patterns, and knitting books. The site has messaging and chat features, as well as a wide range of groups and forums that is growing daily. Knit bloggers can connect their blog to their profile and to specific projects for easy access. For designers and yarn artists, Ravelry features portfolios to display patterns and yarns. Finally, there is the inspiration that can be gained by surfing through the pages of other knitters' work. This innovative site continues to have a positive impact on the knitting and crocheting community, encouraging more of the connections that are at the hearts of these crafts.

My knitting circle is unconventional in that it is a global one. I have one or two local friends to knit with, but the majority of my circle is a collection of friends that I've met through the knit blogging community. Though my knitting circle is spread to the four winds, they are among my closest friends. It doesn't matter that we may not have met face to face or even spoken on the phone. We are in contact daily, always there to offer that extra push to go ahead and start that daunting lace project, the encouragement to finish the throw that threatens to drag on forever, or just to give a pat on the back for a job well done.

For a Sense of Community

Here are just a few places to start exploring the online knitting community.

Knitty.com
www.knitty.com
www.knittyboard.com
Amy Singer started Knitty as an online knitting 'zine in 2004. Knitty features a quarterly newsletter full of patterns, articles, and reviews. Knitty has become a preeminent forum and chat room for those who live and breathe knitting.

Ravelry
www.ravelry.com
Ravelry was developed and launched in 2007 as a social networking site for knitters, but it also includes forums, a growing pattern and yarn database, and places for individual knitters to inventory their yarn, projects, needles, friends, and books. You will need to request an invitation to join and wait until they can process your request, but the momentum is building on this, so you won't wait too long. Trust me, the phenomenon that is Ravelry is definitely worth the wait.

Craftster
www.craftster.org
Craftster is an online community with a hip and young feel. While it is not specifically geared toward knitting or crochet, it does include those crafts in the resources.

Global Baby Layette

by Jacque Landry

The idea for the global baby layette came from a desire to honor the many global knitting relationships and virtual knitting circles that are a part of knitting today. It is designed to be used by all knitting circles, whether they are traditional or transcontinental. The layette features designs appropriate for both beginners and more seasoned knitters. In the blogging world, we are always hearing of a lovely expecting mom or someone who is about to become a grandma, auntie, or uncle. Who better than a fellow knitter to appreciate all the hand-knit goodness provided by a whole layette?

For this design to work as a global project, here are a few suggestions:

- One person becomes the organizer. It is that person's job to recruit knitters willing to commit to one or more of the projects involved.

- Once the organizer has a group assembled, it is a good idea to set up a private blog where the group can discuss decisions and share progress on the projects. A free blog can be set up at *www.blogger. com*, or on Ravelry if the project doesn't hinge on secrecy. The group can collectively choose their yarns and colors and possibly even coordinate where to buy their yarn. They should also agree on a due date for the finished projects.

- Once the projects are complete, the organizer sends an empty basket large enough to hold all the knitted items, as well as a baby card with something similar to the following note: "Mom-to be, be on the lookout for a basketful of special gifts for your special delivery. Wishing you all the best, Your Knitting Friends."

- The organizer can set up a mailing schedule so that the recipient gets a new package every three to four days. Each member of the group can then send their portion of the layette with a note (and any relevant care instructions).

- It's a nice idea to throw in a little something with each knit package:
  1. Diaper bag: Include a package of diapers, wipes, and a tube of diaper cream.
  2. Baby hoodie: It's only a matter of time before baby will be teething, so add a few teething toys to your package.
  3. Baby hat and booties: It's never too early to protect from sun damage, so add some infant sunblock to your gift.
  4. Blanket: Baby may need a cute teddy bear or nightlight for bedtime.
  5. Baby washcloths: Don't forget baby's bath supplies: baby shampoo, body wash, baby powder, and a rubber ducky are a few ideas.
  6. Nursing bibs: Add nursing pads or bottles and a bottle brush.

> It's important that the recipient of a hand-knit item knows the proper way to care for it. A handwritten note on attractive cardstock can be a charming addition to your gift. Provide washing and drying instructions as well as any other care tips regarding specific notions such as buttons. If you are unsure about the best ways to care for the item, refer to your yarn's label for care instructions. Get creative and use rubber stamps, paper punches, and stickers to add a personal touch, or keep it simple with well-chosen paper and colored archival-quality pens. With the variety of crafting supplies available, making coordinating care instructions is a snap.

Baby Uey Diaper Bag

Design by Vyvyan Neel

Most moms I know like to carry a large diaper bag. The idea is to have enough room for the baby's necessities and also some of Mom's stuff. The interior of this bag has an assortment of different sizes of pockets, sure to meet most of Mom's and Baby's needs. The handles are long enough to carry on your shoulder, but also just right for carrying as a handbag. And when Baby is grown up, it can be used as an overnight bag.

Number of Knitters
Two to eight. The bag is worked in 2 pieces that are sewn together, then joined by the bottom; the front flap is sewn to the bag; straps and pockets are worked separately.

Finished Measurements
Before felting: 26" long x 13" deep x 13" high
After felting: 18¹/₂" long x 9¹/₄" deep x 9¹/₄" high

Materials
Yarn
Three colors of worsted weight yarn in a non-superwash animal fiber; all colors should be the same type of yarn to ensure that the pieces felt at a similar rate. The yarn used in the sample is
- Brown Sheep Lamb's Pride Worsted (85% wool/15% mohair; 190 yds/4 oz per skein): 4 skeins Chocolate Soufflé #M151 (A), 3 skeins Jaded Dreams M190 (B), and 2 skeins Cream #M10 (C)
- DMC Cotton Perle 5 (100% cotton; 27.3 yds/5g per hank): 1 hank Dark Brown #938

Needles
Size 8 (5mm) needles (any style) or size needed to obtain gauge; size 10 (6mm) double-pointed, 24" and 32" circular needles

Notions
Size H/8 (5mm) crochet hook, 1 [1¹/₂"] button (JHB #53254 used on sample); 4 [1"] buttons (LaPetite #303 used on sample); 2 pieces 12" x 18" clear plastic canvas (7 mesh); sharp tapestry needle (small enough to fit through button eye while threaded with Cotton Perle)

Gauge
20 sts and 30 rows = 4" (10cm) in Linen st with smaller needles.
16 sts and 32 rows = 4" (10cm) in garter st with larger needles.
Gauge is not critical for the pieces that will be felted; make sure that your sts are loose and airy.

Pattern Stitch
Linen St (odd number of sts)
Row 1 (RS): K1, *yf, sl 1 purlwise, yb, k1, rep from * to last 2 sts, yf, sl 1 purlwise, p1.
Row 2: P1, *p1, yb, sl 1 purlwise, yf, rep from * to last 2 sts, p1, yb, k1.
Rep Rows 1 and 2 for pat.

Pattern Notes

- This bag is worked by making different-sized mitered rectangles. First, 2 long rectangles are worked, then smaller end rectangles are made by picking up stitches along the edges of the longer ones. After these 3-piece rectangles are sewn together into a tube, the bottom is made by picking up stitches along one short side of the bag.
- When working the mitered pieces, always use the Knit-On method of casting on and slip the first stitch of each row knitwise and purl the last st; this will form a neat chained edge into which to pick up stitches.
- To minimize the number of yarn tails to weave in after completing the bag, weave them in at color changes as you knit.
- Tip: Mark the position of the double decrease (SK2P) as follows: Cut a 12" length of smooth waste yarn (cotton works well) for each marked decrease. *On Row 2 (set up marker):* Work the SK2P, then slip the stitch just made back to the left needle; place waste yarn marker between the 2 needles, then slip the stitch back to right needle and continue knitting. *On following WS rows:* Work to 1 stitch beyond the waste yarn marker and slip the last stitch worked back to left needle; flip the waste yarn between needles to the back of work, then slip the stitch back to the right needle and continue knitting. On following RS rows: Work to 1 stitch before waste yarn marker, work SK2P, then slip the stitch just made back to the left needle; flip the waste yarn between the needles to the back of work, then slip the stitch back to right needle and continue knitting.

Instructions

Long Side

Make 2

With A and using Knit-On method, CO 194 sts.

Row 1 (WS): Knit to last st, p1.

Row 2 (RS): Sl 1 knitwise, k46, SK2P, k94, SK2P, k46, p1, placing markers as suggested in Pattern Notes—190 sts.

Row 3 (WS): Sl 1 knitwise, knit to last st, p1, flipping markers as suggested in Pattern Notes.

Row 4 (RS): Sl 1 knitwise, *knit to 1 st before marker, SK2P; rep from * once, knit to last st, p1, flipping markers as suggested in Pattern Notes—186 sts.

Rep Rows 3 and 4 and *at the same time,* change colors as follows:

After working 13 rows total in A (ending with a WS row), *work 12 rows with B, work 12 rows with C, work 12 rows with A; rep from * once more, then work with B until 6 sts remain.

Next row (WS): SK2P twice.

Last row (RS): K2tog, break yarn and pull through loop.

Short Side 1

Make 2, 1 each along the left edge of each Long Side.

With A and using Knit-On method, CO 24 sts, pick up and knit 50 sts along short edge of one of the Long Sides, CO 24 sts—98 sts.

Row 1 (WS): Knit across row to last st, p1.

Row 2 (RS): Sl 1 knitwise, k22, SK2P, k46, SK2P, k22, p1, placing markers as suggested in Pattern Notes—94 sts.

Row 3 (WS): Sl 1 knitwise, knit to last st, p1, flipping markers as suggested in Pattern Notes.

Row 4 (RS): Sl 1 knitwise, *knit to 1 st before marker, SK2P; rep from * once, knit to last st, p1, flipping markers as suggested in Pattern Notes—90 sts.

Rep Rows 3 and 4 and at the same time, change colors as follows:

After working 13 rows total in A (ending with a WS row), work 12 rows with C, work 12 rows with A, then work with B until 6 sts remain.

Next row (WS): SK2P twice.

Last row (RS): K2tog, break yarn and pull through loop.

Short Side 2

Make 2 along the right edge of each Long Side.

Work as for Short Side 1, but change colors as follows:

Begin with C and work 13 rows (ending with a WS row), work 12 rows with A, work 12 rows with C, then work to end with B.

With RS facing, sew Short Sides 1 and 2 together at each end, forming a wide tube.

Base

The base is worked in a "fringed" striped garter stitch.

- The garter stripes are created by knitting 2 rows in 1 color, then sliding the piece to the other end of the needle and purling 2 rows with another color.
- The fringe is created by cutting each color of yarn after working 2 rows; the cut ends are also used to attach the base to the long sides of the bag. Always leave a 4" tail when joining or cutting the yarn.

With RS facing and using circular needle and B, leaving a tail at least 4" long, pick up and knit 48 sts (from right to left) along bottom edge of one of the combined Short Sides.

Row 1: Knit, then break yarn, leaving a 4" tail; slide sts to opposite end of needle; do not turn.

Rows 2 and 3: Leaving a 4" tail, join C and purl 2 rows. Break yarn, leaving a 4" tail, and slide sts to opposite end of needle; do not turn.

Rows 4 and 5: Leaving a 4" tail, join A and knit 2 rows. Break yarn, leaving a 4" tail, and slide sts to opposite end of needle; do not turn.

Rep Rows 2–5, changing colors every 2 rows in following sequence: B, C, A.

Work until base measures 26". BO on 2nd row of a color change, leaving a tail long enough to sew this edge to the bottom edge of the other combined Short Side piece.

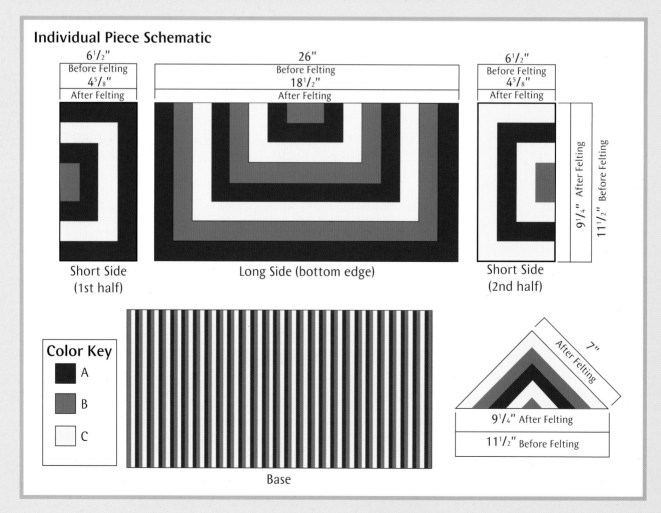

Individual Piece Schematic

Short Side (1st half)

Long Side (bottom edge)

Short Side (2nd half)

Color Key
A
B
C

Base

To attach the loose edges of the Base to the bag, use a crochet hook to pull the 4" tails through the bottom edges of the Long Side pieces. Tie tails together 2 strands at a time in a secure double knot.

Trim yarn tails to approx 2½".

Triangular Top Flap

With C and using Knit-On method, CO 57 sts.

Row 1: Sl 1 knitwise, k2tog, knit to last st, p1—56 sts.

Row 2 (RS): Sl 1 knitwise, k2tog, k24, SK2P, k25, p1, placing marker as suggested in Pattern Notes—53 sts.

Row 3: Sl 1 knitwise, k2tog, knit to last st, p1, flipping marker—52 sts.

Row 4: Sl 1 knitwise, k2tog, knit to 1 st before marker, SK2P, knit to last st, p1—49 sts.

Rep Rows 3 and 4 and at the same time, change colors as follows:

After working 7 rows total in C (ending with a WS row), work 6 rows with B, work 6 rows with A, and 6 rows with C—8 sts rem.

Next row (RS): With B, sl 1 knitwise, k2tog, SK2P, k1, p1—5 sts.

Next row: Sl 1 knitwise, SK2P, p1—3 sts.

Next row: SK2P, then fasten off last st.

Center the long edge of the flap piece to the top center of a Long Side piece and sew together.

I-Cord Edging

With WS facing and using dpns and A, beginning at the center of a top edge of a Short Side, work attached I-cord as follows:

CO 6 sts. Slide sts to opposite end of dpn.

*K5, sl 1 knitwise, pick up and knit 1 st at top edge of bag, psso, slide sts to opposite end of dpn; rep from * across top edge of bag and flap, stopping approx ½" from point of flap.

Button Loop: Work detached I-cord as follows: *K6, slide sts to opposite end of needle; rep from * for 4½".

Begin working attached I-cord as before on opposite side of flap approx ½" from point and continue until you reach beginning of I-cord.

Bind off all sts and break yarn, leaving a 10" tail.

Sew I-cord ends together, then weave in end.

Handle Straps

Make 2

With dpns and A, CO 16 sts and distribute sts onto 3 dpns as follows: 5 sts, 6 sts, 5 sts; join for working in rounds.

Work even in St st (knit all rnds) until piece measures 22".

BO and break yarn.

Interior Pockets

Note: Work all pocket pieces using smaller needles and B.

Pocket 1

Make 3

CO 21 sts. Work in Linen st until piece measures 7", ending with a WS row. BO knitwise.

Pocket 2

Make 1

CO 21 sts. Work in Linen st until piece measures 5", ending with a WS row. BO knitwise.

Pocket 3

Make 1

CO 55 sts. Work in Linen st until piece measures 5½", ending with a WS row. BO knitwise.

Pocket 4

Make 1

CO 71 sts. Work in Linen st until piece measures 7", ending with a WS row. BO knitwise.

Finishing

Weave in any loose ends. Do not attach handles until after felting process.

Felting

Place bag and handles into separate zippered mesh bags or pillowcases; do not felt the pockets. Fill a top-loading washing machine with hot water to lowest water level and add a small amount of detergent. Put the bags or pillowcases into the water and agitate. Check the felting process every 5–10 minutes, and when checking, separate the different fringe colors to keep them from felting together. Reset agitation cycle as necessary to continue felting, then remove pieces when they are the desired size. Do not use the spin or rinse cycle because that could create creases in the fabric that might not come out later. Rinse the pieces in cold water, gently pressing or squeezing out excess water. You may need to tug the bag a little to set back to a rectangular shape. Stuff bag with loose filling such as plastic grocery bags so that it holds its shape while drying, but leave spaces for air circulation. Clothespins can be used to create creases at the sides and bottom, but remove while the bag is still slightly moist or they may leave indentations.

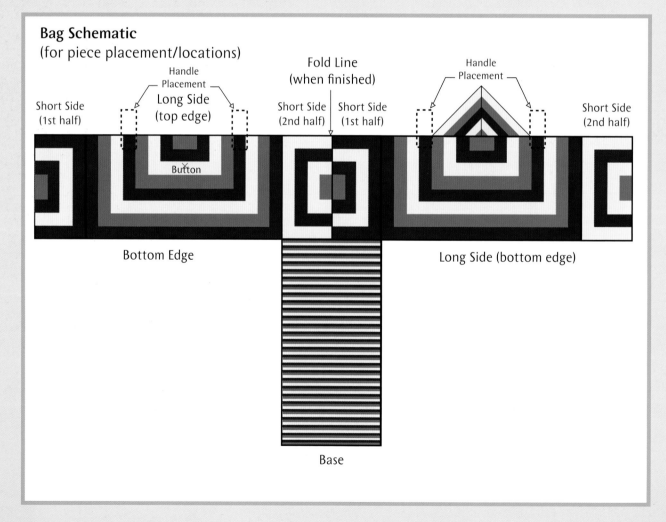

Bag Schematic
(for piece placement/locations)

Fold Line (when finished)

Handle Placement

Handle Placement

Short Side (1st half)

Long Side (top edge)

Short Side (2nd half)

Short Side (1st half)

Short Side (2nd half)

Button

Bottom Edge

Long Side (bottom edge)

Base

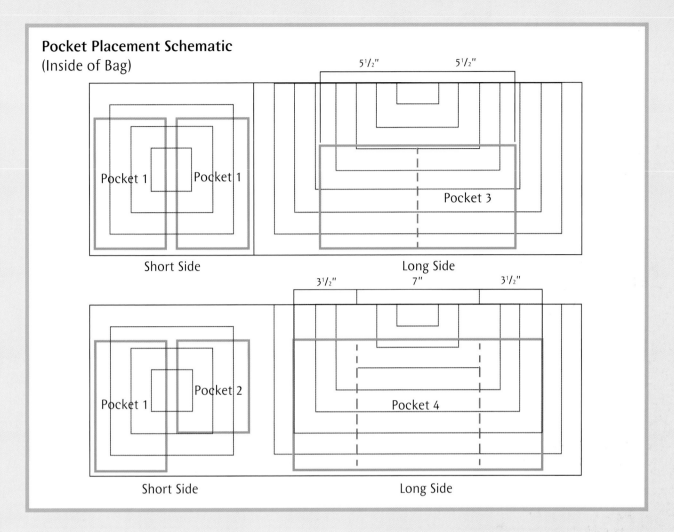

Pocket Placement Schematic
(Inside of Bag)

5¹/₂"   5¹/₂"

Pocket 1   Pocket 1

Pocket 3

Short Side   Long Side

3¹/₂"   7"   3¹/₂"

Pocket 1   Pocket 2

Pocket 4

Short Side   Long Side

Assembly

After pieces are completely dry, use Cotton Perle to sew handles to top edge of bag on either side of the top flap (see picture).

Fold Short Sides 1 and 2 together with right sides together along vertical line where they were stitched together before felting (see Bag Schematic). Hold in place with a clip or pin, if necessary. Place 1 [1"] button on each side of the fold just under the I-cord edging and approx ¹/₂" from fold, and sew the 2 buttons together "cufflink-style" through the 2 thicknesses of the bag, using a sharp tapestry needle and the Cotton Perle. Fasten securely. Do the same on the other Short Side of the bag.

Sew pockets to inside of bag, referring to the Pocket Placement Schematic. When attaching pockets, make sure to sew through only part of the bag thickness to prevent the stitches from showing on the outside of bag. The red dashed lines represent where an extra row of stitching should be added.

Sew larger button to front of the bag using the flap to find correct location. Attach securely using the Cotton Perle, making sure not to stitch through pockets.

Cut 2 [8" x 18"] rectangles from plastic canvas, angling off corners to keep points from poking through corners of bag. Put both pieces on the bottom of the bag for support. *Optional:* Sew both pieces of canvas together to keep them from separating.

Heads, Shoulders, Knees, and Toes

Designs by Jacque Landry

This baby set covers all the bases. *Heads* is a snazzy tricolored hat with fun pom-pom detailing. *Shoulders* is a baby-sized hooded jacket perfect for when Baby is on the go. It features a solid body and hood trimmed in seed stitch. The colorful reverse stockinette striped sleeves with a striped stockinette stitch roll-up cuff can be made to grow with Baby. *Knees and toes,* of course, refers to Baby's shoes. Three simple designs will keep Baby's toes toasty warm while showing off the wee one's budding sense of style. There are sweet Mary-Jane dress shoes for the little ladies, Chuck Taylor® All-Star® Converse made in the solid classic white, and a laid-back Birkenstock-style bootie that can be customized for boy or girl.

Number of Knitters

One to five. The sweater, hat, and booties can each be made by different knitters.

Yarn

Any smooth worsted weight yarn, preferably cotton. The entire sample set (hoodie, hat, and 1 pair of each kind of booties) was made with the following yarn; other requirements for individual elements are included with the patterns:

- Blue Sky Alpacas Dyed Cotton (100% organic cotton; 150yd/100g per skein): 2 skeins Toffee #623 (A) and 1 skein Caribbean #630 (B)
- Blue Sky Alpacas Organic Cotton (100% organic cotton; 150yd/100g per skein): 1 skein Bone #80 (C)

Hat

Sizes

S (M, L) to fit preemie (0–6 months, 6–12 months). Instructions are for smallest size, with larger sizes in parentheses; if there's only 1 number, it refers to all sizes.

Finished Measurement
Circumference: 12 (14, 16)"

Materials

Yarn

1 skein each A, B, C

Needles

Size 7 (4.5mm) and 8 (5mm) needles or size needed to obtain gauge

Notions

Tapestry needle

Gauge

18 sts and 22 rows = 4" in St st using larger needles.

To save time, take time to check gauge.

Pattern Notes

- The hat is worked with vertical stripes. Each color is cast on separately, then on subsequent rows, the stripes are worked using the intarsia method. Use separate balls of yarn for each color and do not carry the yarn across the back; instead, bring the new color being used up and around the yarn just worked; this will "lock" the colors on the WS and prevent holes from occurring at the join.

- When you begin working the body of the hat, reverse the RS and WS of the piece and interlock the yarns at color changes on the other side. This will give an unbroken line of color on the cuff when it's folded up.

Instructions
Cuff

With smaller needles and A, CO 17 (19, 23) sts; change to B and CO 17 (19, 23) sts; change to C and 17 (19, 23) sts—51 (57, 69) total sts. Do not join.

Work in K2, P2 rib for 2½ (3, 4)", ending with a RS row.

Body

Change to larger needles and, beginning with a RS row, work even in St st for 5 (6, 7)", ending with a WS row; remember to change the side on which you are interlocking your yarns at the color change.

Shape Crown

Row 1 (dec): *K1, ssk, knit to 3 sts before end of stripe, k2tog, k1; rep from * to end of row—45 (51, 63) sts.
Row 2: Purl.
Rep [Rows 1 and 2] 6 (7, 9) times more—9 sts rem.
Next row: SK2P across—3 sts.

Break yarn, leaving a tail at least 15" long; using tapestry needle, pull tail through remaining sts and tighten.

Finishing

Sew side seam with tail, working seam on cuff and body from opposite sides of fabric so that seam won't show when cuff is turned up.
Weave in all ends. Block as necessary.

Sweater

Size
0–3 months

Finished Measurements
Chest circumference: 21"
Length: 10$^3/_8$"

Materials
Yarn
2 skeins A, 1 skein each B, C

Needles
Size 8 (5mm) needles or size needed to obtain gauge

Accessories
Stitch holders, tapestry needle

Gauge
18 sts and 22 rows = 4" in St st
To save time, take time to check gauge.

Pattern Note
The hood is cast on in 2 pieces to allow for neck contouring. It is then joined and worked in one piece until the end, when it is again worked in 2 pieces.

Instructions
Back
CO 49 sts.
Work 4 rows in K1, P1 rib.
Work in St st until piece measures 6" from beginning, ending with a WS row.

Raglan Shaping
Row 1 (RS): K1, ssk, knit to last 3 sts, k2tog, k1—47 sts.

Row 2 and all WS rows: Purl.
Row 3: Rep Row 1—45 sts.
Row 5: K1, ssk twice, knit to last 5 sts, k2tog twice, k1—41 sts.
Row 6: Purl.
Rep [Rows 1–6] 3 more times—17 sts.
BO.

Left Front
CO 25 sts.
Work 4 rows in K1, P1 rib, ending with a RS row.
Row 1 (WS): K1, p1, k1, purl to end.
Row 2 (RS): Knit to last 2 sts, p1, k1.
Work even in established pattern until piece measures 6", ending with a WS row.

Raglan Shaping
Row 1 (RS): K1, ssk, work in established pattern to end of row—24 sts.
Row 2 (WS): Work even.
Row 3: K1, ssk twice, work in established pattern to end of row—22 sts.
Row 4: Work even.
Rep [Rows 1–4] 3 more times—13 sts.

Neck Shaping
Continue Raglan Shaping and *at the same time,* BO 4 sts at beg of next WS row, then BO 2 sts at beg of following WS row—4 sts.
BO.

Right Front
CO 25 sts.
Work 4 rows in K1, P1 rib, ending with a RS row.
Row 1 (WS): Purl to last 3 sts, k1, p1, k1.
Row 2 (RS): K1, p1, knit to end.
Work even in established pattern until piece measures 6", ending with a WS row.

Raglan Shaping
Row 1 (RS): Work in established pattern to last 3 sts, k2tog, k1—24 sts.

Row 2 (WS): Work even.

Row 3: Work in established pattern to last 5 sts, k2tog twice, k1—22 sts.

Row 4: Work even.

Rep [Rows 1–4] 3 more times—13 sts.

Neck Shaping

Continue Raglan Shaping and *at the same time,* BO 4 sts at beg of next RS row, then BO 2 sts at beg of following RS row—4 sts.

BO rem 4 sts on next RS row.

Sleeves

With A, CO 43 sts.

Work 2 rows in K1, P1 rib.

Change to rev St st and begin stripes in following sequence: 2 rows each B, C, A.

Continue in established stripe sequence throughout, changing colors every 2 rows, and work even until sleeve measures 6 ³/₄", ending with a RS (purl) row.

Raglan Shaping

Row 1 (WS): K1, ssk, knit to last 3 sts, k2tog, k1—41 sts.

Row 2: Purl.

Row 3: K1, ssk twice, knit to last 5 sts, k2tog twice, k1—37 sts.

Row 4: Purl.

Rep [Rows 3–4] 8 times—7 sts.

BO.

Hood

Right Side

CO 7 sts.

Row 1 (WS): P4, k1, p1, k1.

Row 2: K1, p1, k5, CO3—10 sts.

Row 3: P7, k1, p1, k1.

Row 4: K1, p1, k8, CO4—14 sts.

Row 5: P11, k1, p1, k1.

Place these Right Side sts on holder. Break yarn.

Left Side

CO 7 sts.

Row 1 (RS): K5, p1, k1.

Row 2: K1, p1, k1, p4, CO3—10 sts.

Row 3: K8, p1, k1.

Row 4: K1, p1, k1, p7, CO4—14 sts.

Row 5: K12, p1, k1.

Join Sides

Row 1 (WS): K1, p1, k1, p11, CO12, place Right Side sts from holder onto left needle with WS facing, purl to last 2 sts, k1, p1—40 sts.

Row 2 (RS): P1, k1, p1, knit to last 2 sts, p1, k1.

Row 3: K1, p1, k1, purl to last 2 sts, k1, p1.

Rep Rows 2 and 3 until center back hood measures 6 ³/₄", ending with a WS row.

Shape Top Hood

Next row (RS): P1, k1, p1, k15, k2tog, ssk, k16, p1, k1—38 sts.

Left Side

Row 1 (WS): K1, p1, k1, p16; turn, leaving remaining sts unworked on needle.

Row 2: Ssk, k15, p1, k1.

BO 17 sts, break yarn, then fasten off last st before Right Side sts on hold.

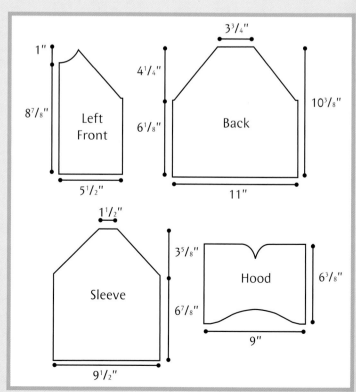

Right Side

With WS facing, rejoin yarn.

Row 1: P17, k1, p1.

Row 2: P1, k1, p1, k14, k2tog—18 sts.

BO, then break yarn, leaving a 20" tail.

Finishing

Block pieces to finished measurements.

Sew raglan, side, and underarm seams. Sew top seam of hood. Sew hood to neck.

Weave in ends.

Booties

Sizes

S (M, L) to fit 0–3 months (3–6 months 6–12 months). Instructions are for smallest size, with larger sizes in parentheses; if there's only 1 number, it refers to all sizes.

Finished Measurements

Foot length: 3 (3½, 4)"

Materials

Yarn

Colors as indicated in individual patterns

Needles

Size 5 (3.75mm) [7 (4.5mm) or 9 (5.5mm)] straight and double-pointed needles or size needed to obtain gauge

Notions

Size H/8 (5mm) crochet hook, stitch holders, stitch markers, tapestry needle, embroidery needle (where needed)

Gauge

Size S: 21 sts and 26 rows = 4"/10cm in St st using size 5 (3.75mm) needles.

Size M: 18 sts and 24 rows = 4"/10cm in St st using size 7 (4.5mm) needles.

Size L: 16 sts and 24 rows = 4"/10cm in St st using size 9 (5.5mm) needles.

To save time, take time to check gauge.

Pattern Notes

- There is 1 pattern for each style; sizes are determined by needle size and gauge.
- All three versions are worked mostly on two needles and feature basic crochet and embroidery.

Instructions: Mary Jane Booties

Yarn: 1 skein each A and C

Cuff

With appropriate-sized needles and C, CO 20 sts.

Work 5 rows in K1, P1 rib.

Shoe Upper and Toe

Row 1 (RS): [K1, p1] 3 times, k8, place rem 6 sts on holder (a large coilless safety pin or waste yarn is good).

Row 2: P8, place last 6 sts on holder.

Work in St st for 10 rows.

Change to A and knit 4 rows.

Sole

Row 1 (RS): K8, then pick up and knit 9 sts along left side of top strip, knit 6 sts from holder.

Row 2: Knit across all sts on needle, yf, pick up and purl 9 sts along right side of strip (inserting needle from back to front to pick up the stitch), yb, k6 sts from holder—38 sts.

Row 3: K13, k2tog, k8, k2tog, k13—36 sts.

Row 4 and all WS rows: Knit.

Row 5: K12, k2tog, k8, k2tog, k12—34 sts.

Row 7: K11, k2tog, k8, k2tog, k11—32 sts.

Knit 4 rows even.

Last row: K16 sts; break yarn, leaving a 24" tail. Join the 16 sts from each needle by grafting or using 3-needle BO. Using remaining tail, sew back seam.

Shoe Strap: Chain 8 sts using crochet hook. Break yarn leaving a 6" tail and fasten off. Tack down strap of shoe across sock area.

Sock Ruffle (optional)

With dpns and A pick up and knit 18 sts at point where ribbing and stockinette meet; place marker and join.

Rnd 1: Knit.

Rnd 2: K1f&b in every st—36 sts.

BO all sts.

Weave in ends.

Instructions: Chuck Taylor® Converse Booties

Yarn: 1 skein C; small amounts of A and B

Cuff

With appropriate-sized needles and C, CO 6 sts, pm, CO 8 sts, pm, CO 6 sts—20 sts.

Row 1 (RS): [K1, p1] to first marker; knit to next marker; [k1, p1] to end.

Row 2: [K1, p1] to first marker; k1, p6, k1 to next marker; [k1, p1] to end.

Rep these 2 rows 4 more times.

Shoe Upper and Toe

Row 1 (RS): [K1, p1] to marker; knit to next marker; place last 6 sts on holder.

Row 2: K1, p6, k1; put last 6 sts on stitch holder—8 sts.

Row 3: Knit.

Row 4: K1, p6, k1.

Rep last 2 rows 4 more times.

Next 4 rows: Knit.

Sole

Work as for Mary Jane Booties.

Embellishments

With RS facing, beginning at back of shoe, working from right to left and using tapestry needle and A, work a line of backstitching (see Glossary) between the first and 2nd garter ridges on the right side of shoe, around toe, then between the 2nd and 3rd garter ridges on left side of shoe; note: this will be one continuous line of backstitching (see photo).

With RS facing, beginning in the middle of one side and using tapestry needle and B, work a line of backstitching between the garter ridges immediately below the previous line, ending at the same position halfway around the other side.

With tapestry needle and a strand of C doubled that is approx 25" long, make "laces" as follows (see photo): Beginning at top of bootie on one side of St st front section, insert needle yarn from WS to RS, *then bring yarn across St st section and insert needle yarn from RS to WS at same point on other side; insert needle from WS to RS couple sts down, then back across to original side and insert needle from RS to WS a couple sts down from previous position; bring yarn from WS to RS a couple sts down; rep from * going back and forth across the St st section until "laces" are a couple sts above toe. Cut yarn and secure both ends.

With B, embroider a small star on the outward facing side of each bootie.

Instructions: Birkenstock Sandal Booties

Yarn: 1 skein each A and B

Cuff

With appropriate-sized needles and B, CO 20 sts. Work 8 rows in K1, P1 rib.

Shoe Upper and Toe

Row 1 (RS): With B, [k1, p1] 3 times, with A, k8; place rem 6 sts on holder (a large coilless safety pin or waste yarn is good).

Row 2 (WS): With A, k8; place last 6 sts on st holder—8 sts.

Row 3: With A, knit.

Rows 4–7: With B, work 4 rows St st, beg with a WS row.

Rows 8–10: With A, purl 3 rows.

Rows 11–14: With B, work 4 rows St st, beg with a RS row.

Shoe Upper and Toe

Row 1 (RS): With B, k8, pick up and knit 9 sts along left side of top strip, alternating between A and B as necessary to match stripes on upper (see photo), then with B, k6 from holder.

Row 2: Purl across working in established colors, then pick up and purl 9 sts along right side of strip (inserting needle from back to front to pick up the stitch), again alternating between A and B as necessary to match stripes on upper, then with B, p6 from holder—38 sts.

Row 3: Working in established colors, k13, k2tog, k8, k2tog, k13—36 sts.

Row 4: Working in established colors, purl.

Row 5: Working in established colors, k12, k2tog, k8, k2tog, k12—34 sts.

Row 6: Cut B; with A only, purl.

Row 7: K11, k2tog, k8, k2tog, k11—32 sts.

Knit 4 rows even.

Last row: K16 sts; break yarn, leaving a 24" tail.

Join the 16 sts from each needle by grafting or using 3-needle BO. Using remaining tail, sew back seam. Weave in all ends.

Sock Ruffle (optional)

Work as for Mary Jane Booties.

Best Baby Blankie

Design by Sharon Vandersar

This is a lovely, soft baby blanket. It is designed for the first months of a newborn's life when a small yet warm blanket is necessary. It is the perfect size to tuck on top of Baby in the car seat, carrier, or stroller. It also makes a cozy pad for laying Baby down. Even when Baby has outgrown this blanket, it makes a great snuggly.

Pattern Notes

- The blanket is worked from the center out, beginning on double-pointed needles and switching to a circular needle once there are about 25 stitches per needle; when switching to circular needle, separate

Number of Knitters

One—part of the layette package

Finished Measurements

20" square

Materials
Yarn

Any soft, baby-friendly worsted weight yarn you please. The sample shown was knit in

- Blue Sky Alpacas Organic Cotton (100% cotton; 150yd/100g per skein): 1 skein Bone # 80 (A)
- Blue Sky Alpacas Dyed Cotton (100% cotton; 150yd/100g per skein): 1 skein each Toffee #630 (B) and Caribbean #623 (C)

Needles

Size 7 (4.5mm) double-pointed [2] and 24" and 32" circular needles, or size needed to obtain gauge

Notions

Size F/6 (4mm) crochet hook, stitch markers (1 in CC for beg of rnd), tapestry needle

Gauge

18 sts and 32 rows = 4" in garter st.

Pattern Stitch
Garter St (in the round)
Rnd 1: Knit.
Rnd 2: Purl.
Rep Rnds 1 and 2 for pat.

stitches into quarters by placing markers where ends of double-pointed needles used to be. As the blanket grows, change to longer circular needles as desired.

- The side edges are worked in 2 colors using the intarsia method; when changing colors, bring the new color from under the old color to lock the stitches and prevent holes. Since this blanket can be reversible without a real "wrong side," as you work each side edge, decide which side of the fabric you are going to twist your colors on; feel free to mix it up on the 4 side edges, but be consistent when working each particular edge.

Instructions
Center Block
Leaving a 5″ tail, CO 12 sts with A and distribute evenly onto 4 dpns; place marker for beg of rnd and join, taking care not to twist sts.

Rnds 1, 3, 5, 7: Knit.
Rnd 2: *K1, M1, k1, M1, k1; rep from * around—20 sts.
Rnd 4: *K2, M1, k1, M1, k2; rep from * around—28 sts.
Rnd 6: *K3, M1, k1, M1, k3; rep from * around—36 sts.
Rnd 8: *K4, M1, k1, M1, k4, p4, M1, p1, M1, p4; rep from * once—44 sts.
Rnd 9: *K11, p11, rep from * once.
Rnd 10: *K5, M1, k1, M1, k5, p5, M1, p1, M1, p5; rep from * once—52 sts.
Rnd 11: *K13, p13; rep from * once.
Rnd 12: *K6, M1, k1, M1, k6, p6, M1, p1, M1, p6; rep from * once—60 sts.
Rnd 13: *K15, p15; rep from * once.
Rnd 14: *K7, M1, k1, M1, k7, p7, M1, p1, M1, p7; rep from * once—68 sts.
Rnd 15: *K17, p17; rep from * once.
Change to B.
Rnd 16: *P8, M1, p1, M1, p8, k8, M1, k1, M1, k8; rep from * once—76 sts.
Rnd 17: *P19, k19; rep from * once.

Rnd 18: *P9, M1, p1, M1, p9, k9, M1, k1, M1, k9; rep from * once—84 sts.
Rnd 19: *P21, k21; rep from * once.
Rnd 20: *P10, M1, p1, M1, p10, k10, M1, k1, M1, k10; rep from * once—92 sts.
Rnd 21: *P23, k23; rep from * once.
Rnd 22: *P11, M1, p1, M1, p11, k11, M1, k1, M1, k11; rep from * once—100 sts.
Rnd 23: *P25, k25; rep from * once.
Rnd 24: *P12, M1, p1, M1, p12; rep from * around—108 sts.
Rnds 25, 27, 29: Purl.
Rnd 26: *P13, M1, p1, M1, p13; rep from * around—116 sts.
Rnd 28: *P14, M1, p1, M1, p14; rep from * around—124 sts.
Change to C.
Rnd 30: *K15, M1, k1, M1, k15; rep from * around—132 sts.
Rnds 31, 33: Knit.
Rnd 32: *K16, M1, k1, M1, k16; rep from * around—140 sts.
Rnd 34: *K17, M1, k1, M1, k17; rep from * around—148 sts.
Rnds 35, 37, 39: Purl.
Rnd 36: *K18, M1, k1, M1, k18; rep from * around—156 sts.
Rnd 38: *K19, M1, k1, M1, k19; rep from * around—164 sts.
Rnd 40: *K20, M1, k1, M1, k20; rep from * around—172 sts, with 43 sts in each quarter.
Rnd 41: Purl.

Side Sections
Designer notes: Here you have a little choice in how you want your blanket to look. I love the contrast line created in garter stitch when purling on the right side or knitting on the wrong side. If the contrast line is used in a purposeful way, it becomes a design element. I worked alternating side edges with the contrast line so there really is no "wrong side" on the blanket. If you don't like the contrast

line, simply begin each side section with the right side facing and knit, referring to the diagram for the color placement. Remember as you work each section to be consistent when twisting the yarn at the color change; you should always twist it on the same side for each particular side section.

Each corner stitch is included in the stitch count of the 2 sections on either side of it. Therefore, when working the first 3 sections, you will be drawing a loop in the corner stitch *but not dropping the corner stitch off the needle* until you work the adjacent section.

Section 1 (no contrast line)
Slip last 21 sts worked to dpn.

Row 1 (RS): With RS facing and using A, draw up a loop in Corner St 1 (the corner stitch that's right before the stitches on the dpn), but leave the corner stitch on the circular needle; k21, switch to B and k21, then draw up a loop in Corner St 4, leaving the corner st on the needle—44 sts with 22 sts in each color.

Rows 2–41: Sl 1 knitwise, knit across in colors as established to last st, p1; twist the colors together *on the WS* at the color change for no contrast line. Cut yarns and slip sts to holder to await edging.

Section 2 (with contrast line)
Row 1 (WS): With WS facing and using dpns and A, beginning at Corner St 1, k22; switch to B and k21; draw up a loop in Corner St 2, leaving corner stitch on the circular needle—44 sts with 22 sts in each color.

Rows 2–41: Sl 1 knitwise, knit across in colors as established to last st, p1; twist the colors together *on the RS* at the color change for a contrast line. Cut yarns and slip sts to holder to await edging.

Section 3 (no contrast line)
Row 1 (WS): With WS facing, using dpns and B, beginning at Corner St 2, p22; switch to B and

p21, draw up a loop in Corner St 3, leaving corner stitch on the circular needle—44 sts with 22 sts in each color.

Rows 2–41: Sl 1 purlwise, purl across in colors as established to last st, k1; twist the colors together *on the WS* at the color change for no contrast line. Cut yarns and slip sts to holder to await edging.

Section 4 (with contrast line)
Row 1 (WS): With WS facing, using dpns and A, beginning at Corner St 3, k22; switch to B and k22, ending with Corner St 4—44 sts with 22 sts in each color.

Rows 2–41: Sl 1 knitwise, knit across in colors as established to last st, p1; twist the colors together *on the RS* at the color change for contrast line. Cut yarns and slip sts to holder to await edging.

Corners
Designer note: You can pick up sts around the corners with either RS or WS facing, depending on whether you want a contrast line showing at the pickup line; the contrast line will show on the side opposite that on which you picked up your sts.

Row 1: With C and working from right to left, pick up and knit 21 sts in the slip-st chain edge of a side section, place marker, pick up and knit 1 in the corner stitch, pick up and knit 21 sts along the slip-st chain edge of adjacent side section—43 sts.

Row 2: Sl 1 knitwise, knit to last st, p1.

Row 3: Sl 1 knitwise, knit to 2 sts before marker, ssk, slip marker, k1, k2tog, knit to last st, p1—2 sts dec'd.

Rep Rows 2 and 3 until 5 sts remain, ending with a WS row.

Next row: Ssk, k1, k2tog—3 sts.

Next row: Sl 1 knitwise, k1, p1.

Last row: SK2P. Fasten off.

Repeat on remaining 3 corners.

Edging

Slip sts from holders to circular needle.

Half Corner: With crochet hook and A held double, beginning at any corner tip, draw up a loop and chain 1 in the corner st, then work single crochet in the same st; [ch 1, sc] in every other slipped stitch across the corner edge to live sts from side section.

Live sts: *With the yarn still held double but using only 1 strand, draw up a loop in the first stitch, then draw up a loop in the next stitch, using the other strand; with both strands, draw a new loop through all three loops on the hook, ch 1; rep from * to end of live stitches.

Corner: [Ch 1, sc] in every other slipped st to corner st; [sc, ch 1, sc] in corner st; [ch 1, sc] in every other slipped stitch to next section of live sts.

Live sts: Work across live sts as before.

Corner: [Ch 1, sc] in every other slipped st to corner st; [sc] in corner st, ch 1; cut A and switch to double strand of B and sc in corner st again; [ch 1, sc] in every other slipped stitch to next section of live sts.

Live sts: Work across live sts as before.

Corner: Work around corner as before without changing colors.

Live sts: Work across live sts as before.

Half Corner: [Ch 1, sc] in every other slipped st to corner st; sc in corner st; draw both colors through loop and fasten off.

Finishing

Weave in all ends. Wash according to manufacturer's instructions. Block to finished measurements.

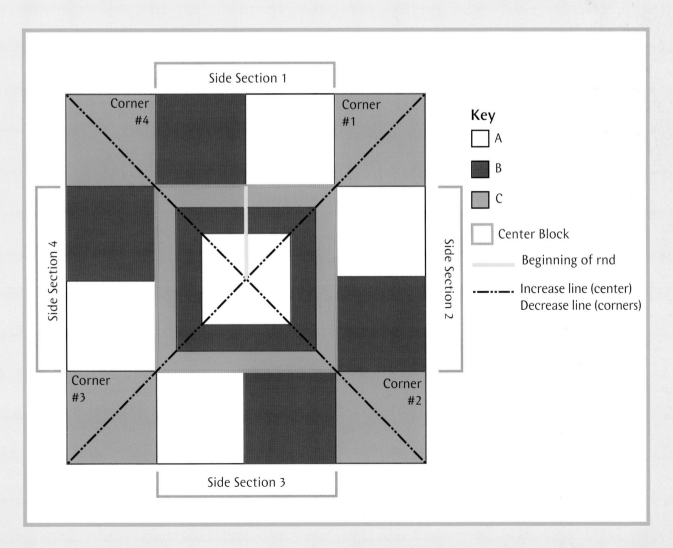

Washcloth Duo

Designs by L. Tippett

Even the tiniest babies need an assortment of accoutrements to accommodate their bathtime needs. These two washcloths are functional and stylish. Dizzy is a reverse stockinette and cable-patterned circular washcloth. Dirty Little Secret is an elegant little washcloth that can be tied up with ribbon to "hide" a bar of soap.

Number of Knitters

One knitter per washcloth. This duo is part of the layette package.

Finished Measurements

Dizzy: Approx 10" diameter
Dirty Little Secret: 10" square

Materials
Yarn

Any smooth, absorbent worsted weight yarn you please. Cotton is best. The samples shown were knitted in

- Blue Sky Alpacas Dyed Cotton (100% cotton; 150 yds/100g per hank): 1 hank each Toffee #623 (A) and Caribbean #630 (B)
- Blue Sky Alpacas Organic Cotton (100% organic cotton: approx 150 yds/100g per hank): 1 hank Bone #80 (C)

If you change up the colors, these 3 hanks will yield 4 washcloths.

Needles

Size 8 (5mm) double-pointed and 24" circular needles

Notions

Cable needle, stitch markers (1 in contrasting color for beg of rnd), tapestry needle, narrow ribbon (optional)

Gauge

18 sts and 22 rows = 4" in St st.
Gauge is not critical for these patterns.

Special Abbreviations

C2B (Cable 2 Back): Slip 2 sts to cable needle and hold in back; k2, k2 from cable needle.
Inc2 (Increase 2 Knitwise): [K1, yo, k1] all in 1 st. This creates a pretty eyelet increase.
Inc2-P (Increase 2 Purlwise): [P1 yo, p1] all in 1 st.

Pattern Notes

- "Dizzy" is worked from the outer perimeter to the center; switch to double-pointed needles when stitches no longer fit comfortably on circular needle.
- "Dirty Little Secret" is worked from the center out to the edge; switch to circular needle when there are enough stitches to do so.

Instructions: Dizzy

With circular needle and B, CO 144 sts; place marker for beg of rnd and join, taking care not to twist sts.

Rnd 1: Knit.

Rnd 2: *P16, p2tog, place marker; rep from * around—136 sts.

Rnd 3: Knit.

Rnd 4: *K4, purl to 2 sts before marker, p2tog; rep from * around—128 sts.

Rnd 5: *K4, purl to marker; rep from * around.

Rnd 6: Rep Rnd 4—120 sts.

Rnd 7: *C2B, purl to marker; rep from * around.

Rep [Rnds 4–7] 5 more times—40 sts.

Next rnd: *Knit to 2 sts before marker, k2tog; rep from * around—32 sts.

Next rnd: Knit.

Rep last 2 rnds twice more, removing markers following last rnd—16 sts.

Next rnd: K2tog around—8 sts.

Next rnd: Knit.

Next rnd: K2tog around—4 sts.

Cut yarn, leaving a 10″ tail; with tapestry needle, draw tail through remaining sts.

Secure tail and weave in ends.

Block.

Instructions: Dirty Little Secret

With A, CO 4 sts. Distribute on 4 dpns, place marker and join, taking care not to twist sts.

Rnd 1: K4.

Rnd 2: *Inc2 in each st around—12 sts.

Rnd 3 (and all odd rounds unless otherwise specified): Knit.

Rnd 4: *K1, Inc2, k1; rep from * around—20 sts.

Rnd 6: *K2, Inc2, k2; rep from * around—28 sts.

Continue in this manner, knitting all odd rounds and working double increase in center st of each dpn on even rnds until there are 25 sts on each dpn—100 sts.

Rnd 25: Change to C and purl around, cut C.

Rnd 26: With A, *p12, Inc2-P, p12; rep from * around—108 sts.

Rnd 28: *K13, Inc2, k13; rep from * around—116 sts.

Rnd 30 (eyelet rnd): *K2, [k2tog, yo, k2] 3 times, Inc2, [k2, yo, k2tog] 3 times, k2; rep from * around—124 sts.

Rnd 32: *K15, Inc2, k15; rep from * around—132 sts.

Rnd 34: Change to C; *p16, Inc2-P, p16; rep from * around—140 sts.

Bind off purlwise with A.

Finishing

Weave in all loose ends. Block. Thread turquoise ribbon through eyelet holes around outer edge and draw up into a little "soap bag" if desired, or leave flat with ribbon as decorative touch.

Oops Uh-Oh Burp Cloths

Design by Darla O'Neal

As a new mother, some of my most valuable possessions were the cloth diapers that I used as burp rags. I carried them everywhere with me and I would have loved to have had something prettier than plain old white cloth diapers. So here's my suggestion: hand-knit burp cloths that can be finished with a crochet border or embellished with embroidery as time allows.

Number of Knitters
One knitter per burp cloth. This is part of the layette package

Finished Measurements
7" x 14" without crochet border, regardless of yarn or gauge used

Materials
Yarn
Any absorbent yarn you please. Cotton is best. The samples shown were knitted in

- Blue Sky Alpacas Dyed Cotton (100% organic cotton; 150yd/100g per skein): 1 skein each Toffee #623 and Caribbean #630
- Blue Sky Alpacas Organic Cotton (100% organic cotton; 150yd/100g per skein): 1 skein Bone #80

Needles
Size 8 (5mm) straight needles, or whatever needles work with your yarn

Notions
Crochet hook for border

Pattern Note
These burp cloths are worked on the diagonal in solid colors with a single crochet border in a contrasting color. This pattern would also look great in a striped pattern sequence of your choice.

Instructions
CO 3 sts.
Row 1: Knit.
Row 2: K1f&b, knit to last st, k1f&b—2 sts inc'd.
Rep Rows 1 and 2 until side edges of piece measure 7".
Row 3: Knit.
Row 4: Ssk, knit to last st, k1f&b—st count remains constant.
Rep Rows 3–4 until long side of piece measures 14".
Row 5: Knit.
Row 6: Ssk, knit to last 2 sts, k2tog—2 sts dec'd.
Rep Rows 5–6 until 3 sts remain.
BO.

Finishing
Weave in any ends.
With a contrasting color, work 1 row of single crochet around the edge of the piece.

Chapter Six
Wrapping Up

Blocking

by Doug Brandt

Why Should I Block?

That used to be a rhetorical question, one I asked myself a lot in the days when I was terrified of blocking. Mostly I just made sure I knitted things that were unlikely to require it—big, baggy sweaters that wouldn't have to conform to my body. In actuality, blocking can solve a small host of problems: Sometimes the pieces just don't look right. The primary function of blocking is to bring a uniformity of shape or size (or both) to your garment, to make all the pieces fit together and look neat and tidy. The knowledge that you can block your garment can mollify that critical parent (either one) stuck to your brainpan, the one who won't stop saying, "You know that thing's not going to fit. Why are you putting time into it?"

If I've had a slight gauge change during the knitting of a garment, say, because I had to put it down for a few months while I worked on some emergency baby garments (why does everyone I know spawn simultaneously?) or I was a little more relaxed after learning a pattern than I'd been during the swatch phase, I know that I can block it to square the pieces, make the back and front the same length and width, make the sleeve caps fit, and so on.

Several of the patterns in this book fit together in puzzle fashion, so having all the pieces—pieces knitted by different knitters, of different yarns—blocked to the right dimensions would really help things along, don't you think?

Here's my basic blocking recipe.

1. First, set up two drying areas. Lay out one or two towels on the bathroom floor. If you have a carpet, spread one or more towels out on the carpet. (If you don't have a carpet, you can buy large pieces of foam core board at an art supply store.

2. In the tub or sink, gently wash your item in lukewarm water and shampoo. You can use regular shampoo, although there are special shampoos just for hand-knit things, like Eucalan. (Never use Woolite! It's quite harsh.)

3. Gently press on the item to squeeze out as much water as possible. Lift the whole thing in a ball—*never* pick it up by an edge, or you'll stretch it out of shape. Lay it gently on one end of a towel and gently (are you seeing the theme?)

spread it out. Roll it in the towel(s) and squeeze out as much of the rest of the water as you can.

4. Again, gently, lift it in a ball and carry it to the other towels. Gently spread it into shape, measuring the edges. Tack the edges down, through the towel into the carpet, using T-pins or blocking pins (you can get them at yarn shops everywhere).

5. Let it dry (a sweater generally dries in twelve hours, so your pieces may take less time if they're not that big).

This process can be hindered by dogs and cats (I'm sure you can imagine how), so if you can, block items in a room that they can be barred from.

Good luck! It's not nearly as scary as it sounds.

For Help with Knitting

Looking for help on the basics or on a specific technique? Here's a list of our favorite how-to reference titles. Also remember that information on knitting techniques can be found on the Internet in blogs, on yarn company websites, and even in video form on YouTube.

The Encyclopedia of Knitting by Lesley Stanfield and Melody Griffiths, published by Running Press, 2000

The Knitter's Companion by Vicki Square, published by Interweave Press, 2006

Knitter's Handbook: A Comprehensive Guide to the Principles and Techniques of Handknitting by Montse Stanley, published by Reader's Digest, 1999

Knitting for Dummies by Pam Allen, published by For Dummies, 2008

Knitting in Plain English by Maggie Righetti, published by St. Martin's Griffin, 2007

Knitting Without Tears by Elizabeth Zimmermann, published by Scribners, 1971

A Treasury of Knitting Patterns, A Second Treasury of Knitting Patterns A Third Treasury of Knitting Patterns, and *A Fourth Treasury of Knitting Patterns* by Barbara G. Walker, published by Schoolhouse Press, 1998

Vogue Knitting: The Ultimate Knitting Book by the editors of *Vogue Knitting Magazine*, 2002

Seams

by Suzyn Jackson

Most of the patterns in this book involve seams of some sort. Here's a primer on sewing knitted pieces together. The technique used will depend on which edges you're sewing together.

Fig. 1

Fig. 2

Fig. 3

Horizontal Seams: Cast-On/Bound-Off Edge to Cast-On/Bound-Off Edge

When properly executed, this technique is nearly indistinguishable from the knitted stitches above and below the seam. This method works best with stockinette stitch, so if you know you'll be joining pieces along their cast-on and bound-off edges, it's helpful to work one or two rows of stockinette stitch at the top and bottom.

First, place the two pieces right side up on a flat surface, abutting as you would like them to be joined. Thread a tapestry needle with a length of the yarn three to four times the length of the seam. Use the yarn that you used in at least one of the pieces.

Starting at the right edge of the fabric if you are right-handed and the left edge of the fabric if you are left-handed, pass the tapestry needle completely behind the first V at the bottom right (left) corner of the top piece. (see Fig. 1) Leave about 6" of yarn hanging, then continue.

Now pass the tapestry needle completely behind the first V at the right (left) edge of the bottom piece. (see Fig. 2) Repeat top and bottom once or twice, then gently pull the yarn until the seam stitches are the same size as the knitted stitches above and below. Your stitches will form a new row that looks like stockinette stitch, with the cast-on and bound-off edges tucked behind it.

Active Edge to Active Edge

This technique is also known as Kitchener stitch, and it is used to join two edges that are still on the needles. The instructions below are for grafting stockinette stitch pieces together.

Holding 2 needles (each holding the same number of stitches) parallel and with wrong sides together:

Step 1: Insert yarn needle *as if to purl* into the first stitch on the front needle and pull yarn through, leaving the stitch on the knitting needle. Insert yarn needle *as if to knit* into the first stitch on the back needle and pull yarn through, leaving the stitch on the knitting needle. (see Fig. 3)

Step 2: Insert yarn needle *as if to knit* into the first stitch on the front needle, and at the same time, let the stitch fall off the knitting needle. Insert yarn needle *as if to purl* into the second stitch on the front needle, and pull through, leaving the stitch on the knitting needle.

Step 3: Insert yarn needle *as if to purl* into the first stitch on the back needle, and at the same time, let the stitch fall off the knitting needle. Insert yarn needle *as if to knit* into the second stitch on the back needle, and pull through, leaving the stitch on the knitting needle.

Repeat Steps 2 and 3 until no stitches remain. When you are done, go back and adjust the size of the grafting stitches so that they match the stitches above and below them.

Mattress Stitch/Vertical Seam: Side Edge to Side Edge

When properly executed, mattress stitch is nearly invisible. This method works best with stockinette stitch, so if you know you'll be joining the side edges of pieces, it's helpful to work one or two stitches of stockinette at the beginning and/or end of each row.

Place the two pieces right side up on a flat surface, abutting as you would like them to be joined. Thread a tapestry needle with a length of the yarn two to three times the length of the seam. Use a fairly smooth yarn in a color similar to the knitted pieces; the yarn used in one of the pieces is fine, so long as it is relatively smooth—don't use specialty yarns such as bouclé.

Starting at the bottom of one of the pieces, look between the first and second stitch—you'll see little horizontal stretches of yarn between and slightly behind the Vs. I'll call these bars. Pass your tapestry needle under the first two bars, leaving a 6" tail. (see Fig. 4)

Now pass your tapestry needle under the first two bars on the other piece. Alternating from one piece to the other piece, continue to pass your tapestry needle under the next 2 bars in succession, tightening the yarn every 4 or 5 stitches. Your seaming stitches will completely disappear, and the two pieces will join up, with the edge stitches on each side tucked to the back. (see Fig. 5)

Cast-On/Bound-Off Edge to Side Edge

This is a combination of the horizontal seam and the mattress stitch. Lay the pieces out, thread your tapestry needle; pick up Vs on the cast-on/bound-off edge and two bars at a time on the side edge. (see Fig. 6) If the number of rows on your side edge isn't exactly twice the number of stitches on your cast-on/bound-off edge, see the section on "cheating" below.

Fig. 4

Fig. 5

Fig. 6

Fig. 7

Whip stitch: Any Edge to Any Edge

While not invisible, whip stitch is an easy way to join two knitted pieces. Holding your two pieces together, put your threaded tapestry needle through both thicknesses, close to the edge, from right to left (left to right if you're left handed). (see Fig. 7) Pull your yarn through, leaving a 6" tail, and repeat. It's not necessary to count stitches, just keep your whip stitches evenly spaced.

Cheating: When Gauges Don't Match

Ask a group of knitters to make 5" squares, and what are the chances each one will have the same number of rows and stitches? Very slim. Let each knitter choose her own yarn, and the chances are even slimmer. Since several of the patterns in this book involve sewing together pieces made by different knitters in dissimilar yarns, you're going to have to deal with variations in gauge.

To solve this problem, you must cheat a bit—seam a couple more stitches here or a couple fewer rows there—to make the joining even.

There are two ways to go about it: calculate, or wing it. I must admit, I tend to wing it, and more than once I've had to remove entire seams when my "guesstimates" were way off. To calculate how often you are going to cheat, you must first figure out the ratio between the two gauges.

For mattress stitch, a cheat means that you pick up only one bar, not two. You'll need to figure out the ratio *in whole numbers* of the row gauges of the two pieces of fabric, with the larger number being an even number.

Example:
- The first piece has a gauge of 4 rows per inch
- The second has a gauge of 5 rows per inch
- So your ratio is 4:5. Since the larger number is odd, multiply both by 2
- Your resulting ratio is 8:10. Now make a little chart to evenly space out 8 stitches against 10 stitches. It will look something like this:

1	2
2	2
1	2
2	2
2	2

Follow this chart as you sew up the seam—always picking up two bars on one side while sometimes picking up one bar on the other.

For a horizontal seam, a cheat means that you skip a V altogether. Determine your stitch gauge ratio in whole numbers.

Example:
- The first piece has a gauge of 4.5 stitches/inch
- The second has a gauge of 5 stitches/inch
- So your ratio is 4.5:5. Since one number isn't whole, multiply both by 2

- Your resulting ratio is 9:10. Make a little chart to evenly space out 9 stitches against 10 stitches. It will look something like this:

1	1	1	1	1	1	1	1	1
1	1	1	1	2 (skip 1)	1	1	1	1

Follow this chart as you sew up the seam, always picking up one stitch on one side and sometimes skipping one stitch on the other.

For a combination horizontal seam/mattress stitch seam, figure out the row gauge on the side edge and the stitch gauge on cast-on/bound-off edge.

- If the number of rows is less than the number of stitches, always pick up a single bar at a time, and sometime skip a V. Example: 4 rows: 5 stitches

1	1	1	1
V	V	VV (skip 1)	V

- If the number of rows is greater than the number of stitches but less than twice the number of stitches, always pick up a V and sometimes pick up one bar instead of two. Example: 9 rows: 5 stitches

2	2	1	2	2
V	V	V	V	V

- If the number of rows is more than double the number of stitches, always pick up a V, and sometimes pick up three bars instead of two. Example: 11 rows: 5 stitches

2	2	3	2	2
V	V	V	V	V

Finally, just remember it's just knitting: It's stretchy, it's forgiving, you can always cheat a few stitches here and there, and anyone in their right mind will only appreciate the love and effort that went into the finished piece.

Abbreviations

approx	approximately
beg	begin, beginning, begins
BO	bind off
CC	contrast color
cm	centimeter(s)
cn	cable needle
CO	cast on
dec(s)	decrease, decreasing, decreases
dpn	double-pointed needle(s)
inc(s)	increase(s), increasing
k	knit
k1f&b (increase)	knit into front then back of same st
k2tog	knit 2 sts together (decrease)
MC	main color
mm	millimeter(s)
M1	make 1 (increase); insert left-hand needle from front to back under the horizontal thread running between stitch just worked and the next stitch; knit into the back of the loop
pat(s)	pattern(s)
p	purl
p1f&b	purl into front then back of same st (increase)
p2tog	purl 2 sts together (decrease)
psso	pass slip st(s) over
rem	remain(s), remaining
rep(s)	repeat(s), repeated, repeating

rnd(s)	round(s)
RS	right side (of work)
rev sc	reverse single crochet (crab st); if right-handed, work single crochet from left to right; if left-handed, work single crochet from right to left
SK2P	slip 1 knitwise, k2tog, psso; a double decrease
S2KP2	slip 2 as if to k2tog, k1, pass slipped stitches over; this is a centered double decrease
sc	single crochet
sl	slip, slipped, slipping
ssk	[slip 1 st knitwise] twice from left needle to right needle, insert left needle tip into fronts of both slipped sts, knit both sts together from this position (left-leaning decrease)
ssp	[slip 1 st knitwise] twice from left needle to right needle, return both sts to left needle and purl both together through back loops (left-leaning decrease)
st(s)	stitch(es)
St st	stockinette stitch; knit on right side, purl on wrong side
tbl	through back loop
tog	together
yf	yarn forward (move yarn from back of work to front between needles)
yb	yarn back (move yarn from front of work to back between needles)
yo	yarn over (wrap the yarn over the right needle as if you were working a knit stitch but without first going into a stitch on the left needle)

Glossary

3-needle bind-off: This is an easy way to join 2 pieces of knitted fabric.

Hold 2 needles parallel with wrong sides together, each needle having the same number of stitches. Insert a 3rd needle knitwise through the first stitch on the front and back needles and knit 1 stitch. *Knit together the next stitch from the front and back needles and slip the first stitch over the 2nd to bind off. Rep from * to the last stitch, then fasten off.

backstitch: Imagine points A, B, C, and D at 1-st intervals along stitch line. Insert tapestry needle through fabric from right side to wrong side at point A, bring it back up at point B, insert again in point A, and bring it back up at point C, insert needle in point B and bring it up at point D. Continue across, going 2 stitches forward and 1 stitch back.

chain (crochet): Make a slip knot and put on hook. *Yarn over and pull loop through loop of knot; repeat from * until chain is desired length. Cut yarn and fasten off last stitch.

Fair Isle (stranded) knitting: A method of knitting with more than 1 color (usually 2). Knit with 1 color while carrying the color not in use across the wrong side of the fabric. Always carry 1 color above the other and 1 color below so that the yarns are parallel on the back. Do not twist them together. When knitting more than about an inch in 1 color, catch the yarn being carried across the back with the yarn being knitted every few stitches so that the floats don't get too long.

French knot: Thread yarn through a tapestry needle and bring the needle up through knitting. Holding the yarn taut with your left hand, wrap the yarn around the needle twice (wrap more times if you prefer a larger knot). Maintaining the tension on the yarn, reinsert the tapestry needle through the knitting near the place where it originally emerged. Pull the yarn and needle through to the underside, making sure to hold yarn taut throughout. Tie yarn ends into a firm knot on the underside of the knitting.

garter stitch: When working flat, knit every row. When working in the round, knit 1 round, purl 1 round.

gauge: A method of measuring the size of stitches. Usually expressed in stitches and rows per 4 inches. A gauge swatch is a small piece of knitting done to test the gauge obtained with a particular yarn and size of needles. The purpose of working a gauge swatch is to ensure that you are making the same-sized fabric as intended by the designer. Save yourself much heartache by testing your gauge before you start and adjusting the size of needles to get the correct gauge.

graft: See Seams (p. 134)

I-cord: A round knitted tube/cord. To create, work as follows: Cast on the number of stitches indicated for the I-cord. *Knit across, but do not turn the knitting at the end of the row. Slip the stitches from the right-hand needle to left-hand needle; repeat from * until the cord is desired length. Bind off. This makes a free-standing I-cord. One can also make I-cords that are incorporated into another fabric; see specific pattern instructions for attached I-cord. If desired, you can also make I-cord on double-pointed needles; after knitting a row, slide the stitches to the end of the needle before knitting the next row.

intarsia: A method of knitting with more than 1 color, with the colors being in separate areas. Also known as "picture knitting." Use separate balls (or bobbins) of yarn for each colored section; do not carry yarns across the back of the fabric. When switching from one color to another, bring the new color being used up and around the yarn just worked; this will "lock" the colors and prevent holes from occurring at the join.

Kitchener stitch: See Seams (p. 134)

knit-on cast-on: Begin with a slip knot on left-hand needle. Knit one stitch through the slip knot, keeping the slip knot on needle and place the stitch just made onto the left-hand needle knitwise. Continue in this manner until desired number of stitches is made.

mattress stitch: See Seams (p. 134)

reverse stockinette (rev St st): Purl on the right side, knit on the wrong side. The resulting fabric is bumpy on the right side and smooth on the wrong side.

ribbing: Alternate knit and purl stitches to form a fabric with vertical ridges. 1x1 ribbing = k1, p1 across; 3x3 ribbing = k3, p3 across.

seed stitch: A noncurling stitch created by knitting the purl stitches and purling the knit stitches as they face you. The resulting fabric has a slightly bumpy texture on both sides.

single crochet edge:
1. Push the crochet hook from front to back at the edge of the fabric.

2. While holding the yarn behind the piece, grab it with the hook and pull it back through. You should now have one loop on your hook.

3. Use the hook to reach over the edge of the knitting and grab the yarn again. This time, pull the yarn through the loop that is already on your hook. Again, you have one loop on your hook.

4. Push the hook through the next space on your fabric (you may have to skip a stitch for proper spacing), grab the yarn, and pull it through the piece. You now have two loops on your hook.

5. Grab the yarn again and pull it through both loops. You now have one loop on your hook.

6. Repeat from Step 4.

When rounding corners, you should work a chain stitch between single crochet stitches as you round the point.

turn: Turn your knitting around to work in the opposite direction.

weave in tails: Using a tapestry needle, pull the loose end of yarn through several loops on the wrong side, then clip the ends.

weave in as you go: Use when changing color or to secure loose tails of yarn as you work. Making sure the tail is on the wrong side, work a stitch, take the yarn tail from under the working strand of yarn and lay it over the top from left to right; drop the tail and work the next stitch, making sure not to catch tail in stitch; bring the yarn tail back over top of working yarn as before except from right to left. Continue in this manner for at least 2 inches or until the tail is secure.

whip stitch: See Seams (p. 136)

Contributors

Doug Brandt learned to knit because of a crush and has been doing so off and on (knitting, not crushing) since the mid-1980s. He has a terrible habit of choosing ridiculously complicated sweater patterns, which means he doesn't make a lot of his own clothes, although he has a closet full of Starmores. He and his wife, Kathy, are the proud parents of Babar, their chinchilla, and Ed, their carnivorous frog. Doug can be reached at dougbrandt1@gmail. com or *www.myspace.com/dougbrandt*.

Laura Brown spends her days chasing after her daughter and awaiting the impending arrival of her son. All her other time is devoted to ignoring chores and knitting as much as possible. She blogs at *http://babyknits.blogspot.com*.

Rachel Cottone is a freelance writer and the daughter of a committed knitter. Rachel currently works in the New York City area and lives in New Jersey with her husband and two beautiful daughters.

Greta Cunningham is a newscaster and reporter for Minnesota Public Radio. She learned to knit in a community education class taught by a World War II veteran. Greta's essay about this knitting adventure is featured in the book *Knitting Yarns and Spinning Tales*, published by Voyageur Press.

Kelley Dean-Crowley taught herself to knit in 2001, taught herself to spin in 2002, and is now working on a book on solar dyeing. She has two kids, two cats, twelve fleeces, and a wonderful husband who just shakes his head at the wonder of it all. Kelley can be found at *www.ceallachknits.blogspot.com* or *www.ceallachdyes.com*.

Meira Drazin has been crocheting since she was eight and learned how to knit around the same time, although she only became a real knitter in her mid-twenties. People never fail to be amazed at how strangely she holds the needles and yarn of both crafts, which is mostly the legacy of being the righty daughter of a left-handed mother (who taught her how to crochet going in the other direction). Meira especially loves knitting children's clothes, and after many years of outfitting her friends' and family's children, she cried the first time she put her own daughter in something she had created with her own hands. Meira is a freelance writer based in Manhattan.

Cindy Goldman is an original member of House of Dreams' Pretty Kitty Knitty Committee. While steadily improving, her knitting skills at present run to hats, scarves, and catnip-stuffed toys for the shelter's annual autumn bazaar. Her goal is to successfully complete one of the charming sweaters from the books written by her knitting mentor, Kristin Spurkland.

Sue Hawley was a teacher and later a teacher of teachers, as well as a poet, watercolorist, weaver, and knitter. For her, art was about the process, not the product (the journey, not the arrival). She realized that warping her loom was weaving, not just getting ready to weave. She was happy to pull out an almost-completed sweater when she noticed a mistake back in the third row, noting that the person she was knitting for probably wouldn't go naked anyway. She died of ALS in 1999.

Cici Heron DeNovo learned the basics of crochet when she was about ten but only started learning in depth and with real enthusiasm a few years ago. She enjoys making small items—catnip mice, hats, mitts, animals—where she can experiment with new stitches and patterns. She's interested in converting and adapting knit patterns to crochet and plans to design her own hats and sweaters. She can be reached at ceci2@oregonfast.net.

Yin Ho learned to knit at a party and was hooked by the colors at the local yarn shop. Her mother still shames her in speed and efficiency, though.

Suzyn Jackson learned to knit from Episcopalian nuns in third grade. She started designing knitting patterns in college so that she could reuse yarn ripped from Goodwill sweaters. Her work has been published in two previous anthologies from Voyageur Press and on Knitty.com. She lives in Maryland with her husband and two gorgeous sons.

Five years ago, *Tracy Sprowls Jenks* started knitting to feed her spiritual and creative side. She also wanted to make things that she could see actually growing and becoming something unique and special. While she enjoys knitting for herself and family, she particularly enjoys making things for others. Tracy attends a lot of meetings and always has her knitting on hand! Contact her at usr.dre@verizon.net.

Jacque Landry was introduced to fiber arts around the age of eight, when her grandmother first taught her to crochet. Many years spent crocheting afghans while dreaming of sweaters prompted Jacque to teach herself to knit. She has never looked back. She is an enthusiastic designer with patterns published in online magazines Knitty.com, Magknits, and Knotions. She designs for Shokay, for One Planet Yarn and Fiber, and on her website at *www.jacquelynlandry.com.* Contact her at jacque@jacquelynlandry.com.

Mary Langevin has been interested in creative adventures since she was a child. Although she pursues many interests, knitting is her passion. She collects yarn not only for her own projects, but also for others' as well. Mary and her husband continue to restore their urban gem in Marble Hill, a Manhattan neighborhood on the Bronx side of the river.

Michele Meadows learned to knit at the age of five, while accompanying her mother on Saturdays to her needlework shop. Soon afterward, she began designing Barbie doll clothes. She is now a true Northern girl, balancing time outdoors—hiking, biking, and kayaking—

with work in her own wool store, Muskoka Yarn Connection. Her passion for knitting has led to teaching and design work for yarn companies and magazines. Michele can be reached at michele_meadows@bellnet.ca, and her company website is muskokayarn.com.

Vyvyan Neel has been a serious knitter for the past five years, but has known the craft since she was taught by her mother as a senior in high school. Now if a day goes by without picking up the needles, she feels like something is missing. She enjoys learning new techniques when she can but considers modular knitting one of her favorites. She blogs at *www.fishbonedesigns.net* and can be contacted at vyvneel@sbcglobal.net.

Darla O'Neal is a stay-at-home mom and a full-time college student. Other than knitting, she enjoys reading, watching television and movies, and spending time with her husband and two little girls.

After earning her apparel design degree from Bassist College in Portland, Oregon, in 1998, *Kristin Spurkland* chose to pursue a path in knitwear design with a focus on hand knitting. In addition to her work for knitting magazines and yarn companies, she is the author of four books: *Knits From the Heart, Crochet From the Heart,* and *Blankets, Hats, and Booties* (Martingale & Co); and *The Knitting Man(ual)* (Ten Speed Press).

When not knitting, Kristin volunteers at House of Dreams Cat Shelter, practices yoga, and takes lessons in hip hop, samba, and Afro-Cuban/Afro-Brazilian dance. She also enjoys reading and cooking, and time spent doing nothing at all. Kristin can be contacted via her websites: *www.kristinspurkland.com* and *www.theknittingmanual.com.*

L. Tippett began knitting at seven years old but only recently picked up her needles again for some "serious" knitting. Now her stash is verging on uncontrollable. She lives in Germany with her husband, two cats, and a dog, and she is learning German in order to better communicate with LYS owners.

Graham Turnbull grew up in Canada but now lives in London, England. He got into knitting as part of his training to be a Waldorf teacher. He confesses that it took him years to learn, but he can teach an eight-year-old to knit in five minutes. He is currently working as an account manager for a Canadian software company. In his spare time, he enjoys singing with the Hackney Singers and taking in neighbors' plants and restoring them to health. Graham can be contacted at graham.turnbull@mac.com.

Sharon Vandersar resides in the Niagara Region of Ontario, Canada, and has been knitting on and off since she was seven or eight. She is a recent convert to Continental knitting and has been crocheting for years. Currently she is fascinated with the sock-making process. She is a single mother of two precious daughters and spends her days working with income tax. This is her first design. She blogs at *www.3redgurlz.blogspot.com* and can be contacted at svandersar@cogeco.ca.

Index